Brain Research and Learning Theory

Brain Research and Learning Theory

Implications to Improve Student Learning and Engagement

Perry R. Rettig and Toni M. Bailey

ROWMAN & LITTLEFIELD
Lanham • Boulder • New York • London

Published by Rowman & Littlefield
An imprint of The Rowman & Littlefield Publishing Group, Inc.
4501 Forbes Boulevard, Suite 200, Lanham, Maryland 20706
www.rowman.com

86-90 Paul Street, London EC2A 4NE

Copyright © 2024 by Perry R. Rettig and Toni M. Bailey

All rights reserved. No part of this book may be reproduced in any form or by any electronic or mechanical means, including information storage and retrieval systems, without written permission from the publisher, except by a reviewer who may quote passages in a review.

British Library Cataloguing in Publication Information Available

Library of Congress Cataloging-in-Publication Data

Names: Rettig, Perry Richard, author. | Bailey, Toni, author.
Title: Brain research and learning theory : implications to improve student learning and engagement / Perry R. Rettig and Toni M. Bailey.
Description: Lanham, Maryland : Rowman & Littlefield, 2024. | Includes bibliographical references.
Identifiers: LCCN 2023037719 (print) | LCCN 2023037720 (ebook) | ISBN 9781475868821 (cloth) | ISBN 9781475868838 (paperback) | ISBN 9781475868845 (ebook)
Subjects: LCSH: College teaching--Methodology. | Cognitive learning theory. | Cognitive neuroscience. | Brain.
Classification: LCC LB2331 .R489 2024 (print) | LCC LB2331 (ebook) | DDC 378.1/7--dc23/eng/20230912
LC record available at https://lccn.loc.gov/2023037719
LC ebook record available at https://lccn.loc.gov/2023037720

Brain Research and Learning Theory: Implications to Improve Student Learning and Engagement took the better part of two years to prepare. But even more, it took a professional lifetime of teaching experience, for the both of us, to research and write. As such, we have received a lifetime of support from our loved ones. This book is dedicated to our spouses.

Dr. Jeri-Mae Astolfi, a highly acclaimed and successful professor and piano performer in her own right, has been a sounding board of ideas and reflections for Perry for the past twelve years. We have discussed our successful approaches in the classroom, as well as those that needed adjustments. We'll never get to that perfect classroom experience or semester, but the struggles have always been worth it.

Mr. Cline Bailey, a critically thoughtful individual who practices in the arts and philosophy, has continued to inspire Toni in her work through deep analytical conversations on society and its connections to how we grow and learn. At the end of these conversations, we do not come to universal truths but truly richer understandings of what it means to be human.

Of course, this book is dedicated to all those current and future professors who strive on a daily basis to provide the best learning experience possible for your students. You are charged with the amazing responsibility of providing the leaders of tomorrow with efficient skillsets for the sake of furthering civility. Therefore, an understanding of how individuals learn, both theoretically and practically, is a critical need. We dedicate this book to your dedication—your triumphs and struggles and your professional ethos in whatever your content area. All our students benefit from your dedication, professionalism, and ethic.

Contents

Acknowledgments	ix
Preface	xi
Introduction	1
Part I: The Brain	11
Part II: Learning Theory	39
Part III: Implications and Applications	57
Bibliography	101
Annotated Bibliography	107
About the Authors	111

Acknowledgments

A book like *Brain Research and Learning Theory: Implications to Improve Student Learning and Engagement* can only be written with the help and direct involvement of many professionals. Dr. W. Joseph Herring, MD, PhD, of the Johns Hopkins School of Medicine and Merck Research Laboratories and Dr. Bermans J. Iskandar, MD, of the Department of Neurological Surgery at the University of Wisconsin both vetted the brain research material covered in Part I. Ms. Lisa Brookshire provided administrative support and was responsible for formatting a number of the manuscript's figures in Part I. Together, these professionals helped to make this book come to life in meaningful and relevant ways.

In a very real sense, we need to acknowledge the dialogue and experiences we have shared over the years with our undergraduate students and with our graduate students who have maintained their regular teaching duties all while pursuing advanced degrees. Along with our own professor colleagues, these conversations only strengthened our understanding of how people learn and how we teach, as well as provided the impetus for writing this book. In addition, we need to acknowledge Dr. Howard Gardner for his work on conceptualizing intelligence as a multifaceted system of *ways of knowing* and Dr. Zaretta Hammond for her inspiring work on culturally responsive teaching and the brain.

It is with the help and guidance of all these individual and collective people we present *Brain Research and Learning Theory: Implications to Improve Student Learning and Engagement*.

Preface

Brain Research and Learning Theory: Implications to Improve Student Learning and Engagement is written by professors for professors. We are life-long educators, having worked in both K–12 and higher education settings our entire careers. We teach, among other topics, undergraduate and graduate courses titled, Learning and Cognition designed for school teachers and leaders. It is from these perspectives that we share our experiences and insights.

"'Learn' is an active verb," according to the National Academies of Sciences, Engineering, and Medicine.

> It is something people do, not something that happens to them. People are not passive recipients of learning. . . . Instead, through acting in the world, people encounter situations, problems, and ideas. By engaging with these situations, problems, and ideas, they have social, emotional, cognitive, and physical experiences, and they adapt.[1]

K–12 educators are steeped in learning theory and brain research as each applies to school classrooms. While college professors are experts in their content fields, most have little formal training in learning theory and recent findings about how the brain learns, processes information, thinks, and makes decisions. The aim of this book is to share insights about the brain and of the learning theories that educators use to inform their pedagogy.

Throughout this text there are many mentions of the word *pedagogy* to emphasize the art and science of teaching. Although the etymology of the term pedagogy indicates its roots in teaching children, the term has expanded over time to indicate the teaching of all ages. While some argue that teaching children and teaching adults are two separate processes, others have argued that they are fundamentally similar.[2]

We accept the latter of these two positions. Yes, there are obvious differences between adults and children such as age, abilities, and experiences, but the capacity for learning is essentially a never-ending process.[3] "It is usually risky to make generalizations about behavior based solely on age."[4] Both children and adults continuously experience events in their lives that they learn from. Additionally, at various points in all our lives, we take on a variety of passive and active learner roles as we negotiate and navigate different learning situations. Therefore, this book is written not from a largely technical and jargon-filled standpoint but, rather, through the lens of college instructors in a very approachable fashion.

While, undoubtedly, a myriad of good illustrations exists at colleges and universities across the nation, we will provide examples from our own experiences. Education faculty often refer to three levels of learning reflection: the What? the So What? and the Now What? The What is the actual knowledge or skills that the professor teaches—it's "the stuff" of content. The So What is the general implications of what the students have learned in the classroom. The Now

What is the actual application and higher order thinking of what the students have learned in the classroom and are able to do.

Moving along from content to application is the intent of this book. Our ultimate aim, then, is to help college instructors to reflect upon their teaching. As such, with new understanding about brain research and learning theory, professors can examine their classroom environments, how they construct their lessons, the assignments they give, and how they assess their students' learning as well as the effectiveness of their own instruction.

It is our hope that this book becomes a starting point for individual and group reflection. Academic departments and campus-wide centers for teaching and learning can begin in earnest the dynamic dialogue necessary to provide the best instruction we can for our students. Such efforts would be congruent with the origins of Ernest Boyer's *Scholarship Reconsidered: Priorities of the Professoriate*[5] where teaching and research inform one another in a symbiotic relationship in college classrooms across the nation.

NOTES

1. National Academies of Sciences, Engineering, and Medicine, *How People Learn II: Learners, Contexts, and Cultures* (Washington, DC: The National Academies Press, 2018), 12, https://doi.org/10.17226/24783. The authors go on to indicate: "Many kinds of learning are promoted when the learner engages actively rather than passively, by developing her own models, for example, or deliberately developing a habit or modeling an observed behavior" (67).

2. Malcolm Knowles, *The Adult Learner: A Neglected Species* (Houston: Gulf Publishing, 1973).

3. Geraldine Holmes and Michele Abington-Cooper, "Pedagogy vs. Andragogy: A False Dichotomy," *Journal of Technology Studies* 26, no. 2 (2000): para. 3.

4. Holmes and Abington-Cooper, "Pedagogy vs. Andragogy," para. 3.

5. Ernest Boyer, *Scholarship Reconsidered: Priorities of the Professoriate* (Princeton, NJ: Princeton University Press, 1990).

Introduction

All K–12 educators have Bloom's Learning Taxonomy and Maslow's Needs Hierarchy committed to memory. Both Abraham Maslow and Benjamin Bloom created models to help educators understand how people are motivated to learn and achieve, and the different levels of learning, respectively.

Maslow's Needs Hierarchy clearly visualizes and describes the levels of people's motivation from the most basic to the most advanced (see Figure I.1). Implications for the classroom setting and for pedagogy are enormous. We will find that the onus for motivation moves more from the teacher to the student the higher we travel up the hierarchy.

Maslow's pyramid model contends that individual people are motivated by an ever-increasing hierarchy of needs. Starting at the bottom of the pyramid, people are motivated to take care of their most basic physiological needs—for example, food and water. Once these needs are sufficiently met, the next level people seek is their own safety and security. If the individual's most basic needs are met and they feel safe, they are then motivated by a sense of love, belonging, and acceptance by others.

Once these lower-level needs are met, people are motivated by esteem and then ultimately by self-actualization. The former is a sense of self-esteem and recognition by peers. The final level includes a sense of becoming whole, having personal autonomy, and self-direction. As the model suggests, each of us strives to move higher up the pyramid and are typically not satisfied by the primary levels.

Hastings and West expressed the need for students to take ownership of their own learning because it provides direction and focus for their learning. In other words, students are motivated to actively achieve goals that they establish for themselves, to put forth the energy in the attainment of those goals and to persevere when obstacles are in the way.[1]

We can, however, slip back down the motivation pyramid at any time. For example, should a person's house be destroyed, they could slip from esteem needs to physiological needs. Similarly, a highly self-motivated professional might be given very unique and demanding new job responsibilities and subsequently slip down the hierarchy in the short-term until they regain confidence and expertise. An example many professors might experience is that of moving from teaching face-to-face with content they have mastered to now teaching online.

Unknown to most educators, Maslow had begun work on a more elaborate model, but his work was never published because of his untimely death. However, Figure I.2 highlights these enhanced levels.

Maslow's final, yet unpublished model expanded to include: Cognitive, Aesthetic, and Transcendence levels of need. The former two are immediately after Esteem and just prior to Self-Actualization. Transcendence had now usurped Self-Actualization as the penultimate level.

People are most motivated and compelled to transcend in life through their values to be interconnected with nature and with others. This is where we get the most out of ourselves and the most out of our organizations—when we relate and connect with one another to meet our common goals and mission. It is not a selfish self-actualization—it is beyond that. It is transcendent self-actualization with the whole. Other derivative versions of Maslow's Needs Hierarchy have subsequently been created—mostly as they relate to the work environment, but for the sake of pedagogical discussion, Maslow's original hierarchy remains prescient. This work will be discussed and explicated at length in Part III.

On the other hand, Benjamin Bloom focused his conceptual research on levels of learning, from the most basic to the most advanced. We'll find that much of what we teach and assess in today's classrooms would be considered lower-level Bloom. The lower levels are critical and foundational learning, but they are far from sufficient. Further, many standardized and IQ tests focus at lower levels on Bloom's learning taxonomy.

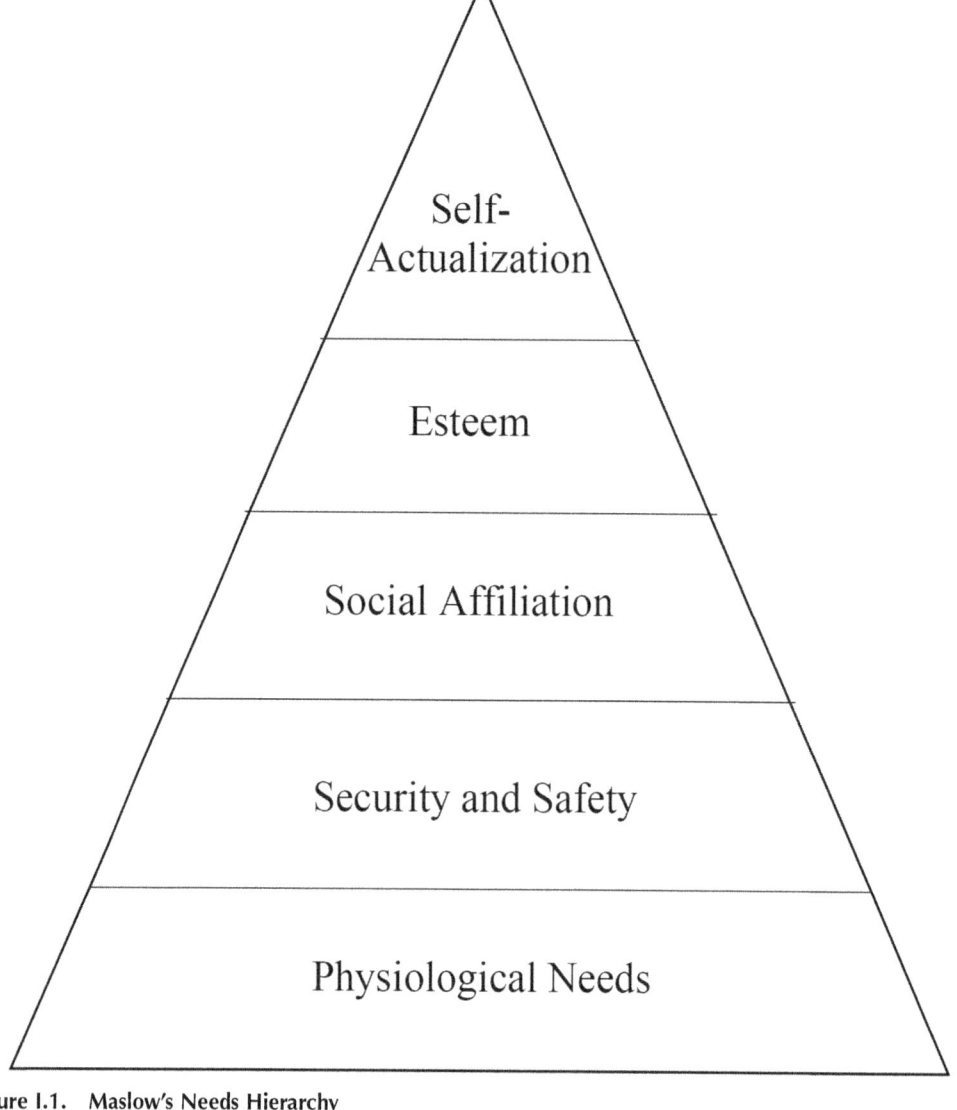

Figure I.1. Maslow's Needs Hierarchy

Bloom and his colleagues published his cognitive learning taxonomy in 1956.[2] This taxonomy has been reimagined,[3] and derivatives[4] have been created over the years, but it remains the foundation of many good instructors' lesson-planning. The original version was considered a more static list of objectives, while newer versions are more dynamic and help to describe what learners actually do. (See figure I.4).

We'll see later in this book that while learning is not linear, perhaps the taxonomy need not be viewed as such either. As learning is dynamic and integrated across domains, so too should the taxonomy be considered dynamic and integrated. An organic or circular depiction may serve as a better visualization.

The lowest level of the revised Bloom's Taxonomy (see Figure I.4) is "Remember," or to recall basic facts and concepts. This is followed by the higher level of "Understand," or to explain ideas and concepts. The next level is "Apply," or to use information in new situations, followed by "Analyze," or to draw connections among ideas. In the revised taxonomy, "Evaluate" is now the next level where students justify a position or decision. The highest level is "Create," where the student is expected to produce new or original work. Again, the implications of this model can be profound with respect to where we focus our time and attention, what we expect of our learners, how we teach them, what assignments we give, and how we assess what they have learned.

This seminal theoretical work provides the baseline for *Brain Research and Learning Theory*. Part I is devoted entirely to brain research—what we know about how the brain works in terms of taking in information, incorporating memories, and how it analyzes, synthesizes, organizes, evaluates, and creates. These understandings directly impact how we teach our content, the classroom environment we create, the kinds of assignments we give, and how we assess our students' learning and the effectiveness of our teaching.

For example, we will find that "the brain is poorly designed for formal instruction,"[5] at least in the way many instructors teach today. Learning is not isolated to one region; the learning

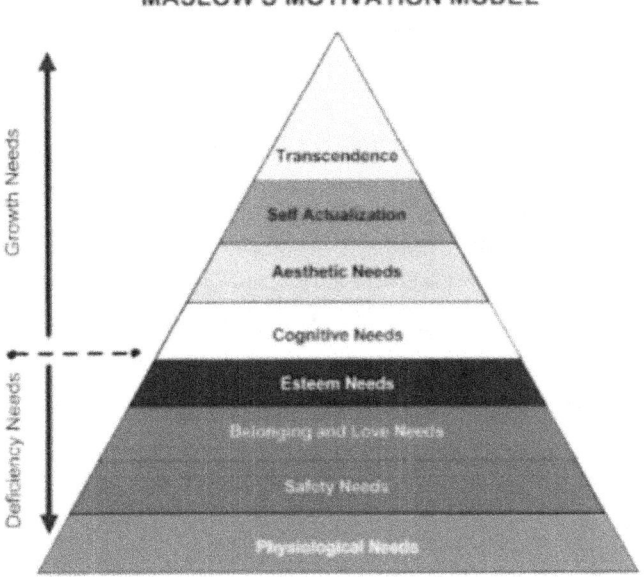

Figure I.2. Maslow's Unpublished Elaborated Hierarchy
Source: Saul McLeod, "Maslow's Hierarchy of Needs," *Simply Psychology*, May 21, 2018, https://www.simplypsychology.org/maslow.html.

process is diffuse across the brain. Also, an adult's attention span is roughly twenty to thirty minutes. We know that students are motivated the most by work they find relevant, meaningful, and relatable to their own experiences—something not often connected to in the typical college classroom. One example of the paradox concerning traditional classroom planning is that the work world our students will enter is computer driven and production oriented, but our classrooms are too often paper-and-pencil driven and exam oriented.

We have learned that "intelligence is plastic and modifiable. All of our experiences result in the formation of neuronal circuits. The richer, more varied, and more challenging the experiences, the more elaborate the neuronal circuits,"[6] according to Richard Restak. Using only one mode for teaching misses the mark for many students, because the orthodox model of learning is often teacher centered and based on authoritarian principles, and it leaves out numerous opportunities for better integration.

In expressing frustration with her own early teaching experiences, Laurie Materna quips:

> You could say that these students were a captive audience in the traditional instructional paradigm, where teachers primarily used the didactic lecture method of disseminating volumes of information to large numbers of students. There was certainly a disparity between the learning style of the students and the teaching style of most of the instructors . . . I knew there had to be a better way to reach these students.[7]

On the other hand, according to Robert Sylwester:

> Imaginative teachers have always used multiple approaches to the curriculum in order to open as many cognitive doors as possible. They presented information to students via one intelligence

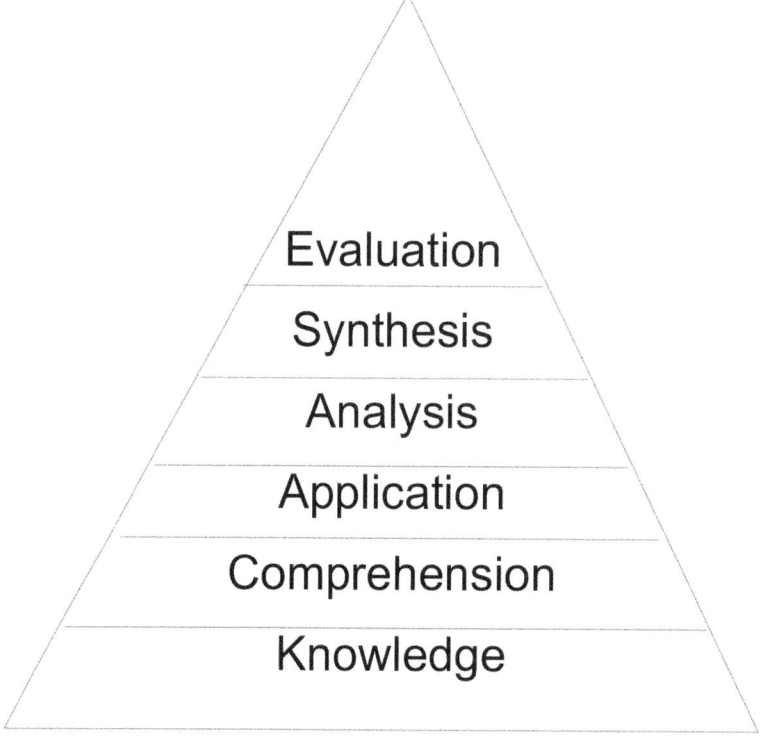

Figure I.3. Bloom's Original Learning Taxonomy

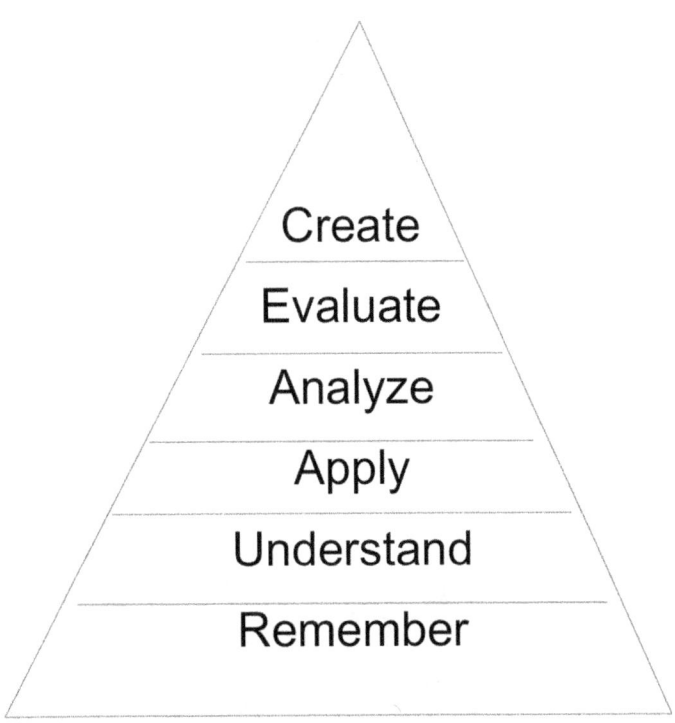

Figure I.4. Bloom's Revised Learning Taxonomy

and then challenged them to paraphrase it using another. They developed open-ended projects that encouraged students to explore multiple approaches to the problem. They encouraged students with different interests and abilities to work together.[8]

With respect to how the human brain grows and matures, we know that the primal reflexive brainstem develops first, followed by the emotional centers in the amygdala, and eventually the thinking portion of the brain—the neocortex. This development takes place even into adulthood for our college students. The human adult brain uses 20 percent of the body's energy, while an infant's consumes up to 65 percent.[9] Babies are born with virtually all the neurons they will ever need, but what they need most of all is neuronal connections—the place where learning happens. In other words, infants are born ready to do anything, they just need the experience.

Good teachers create cognitive dissonance by making students cognitively uncomfortable, so they feel motivated to learn, to understand. The classroom needs to be a place of high challenge, but lower stress. Stress impedes the brain's ability to learn. "Listen first to understand and then to be understood" is the mantra of the best college classrooms. Students need to take on a sense of ownership and responsibility for their own learning and begin to worry less about what the teacher wants or what's on the test. They need to develop a sense of self-motivation, a desire to learn, and a practice of reflective metacognition.[10] "[Researchers] have consistently found that most extrinsic motivators [teacher-driven] damage intrinsic motivation."[11]

Again, Materna explains: "Indeed, the avoidance of threat and bodily harm, the search for emotionally satisfying experiences, and the innate need for novelty and stimulation are the driving forces behind learning."[12] These are the attributes of the best college professors and the classroom environments they try to create where students engage in their learning by taking ownership and strive for higher-order thinking, application, and reflection.

Figure I.5. Circular Model of Bloom's Taxonomy
Source: Created by Dr. Toni Bailey.

Part II then takes us into the realm of learning theory. We'll explore insights from behavioral, cognitive, and social constructivist approaches to learning. These theories will include the work of noted theorists such as Skinner, Bandura, Piaget, Vygotsky, and Booker T. Washington. Diversity, learner growth and development, and environment all have clear implications for our students, as we will see. In 2018, the National Academies of Sciences, Engineering, and Medicine noted: "Each learner develops a unique array of knowledge and cognitive resources in the course of life that are molded by the interplay of that learner's cultural, social, cognitive, and biological contexts."[13]

Like Part I, Part II will conclude with descriptions of implications for our teaching, our classroom environment, the syllabus, the assignments we give, and how we assess both our students' learning and the effectiveness of our own teaching. Parts I and II focus on the What—What are the key concepts from brain research and from learning theory? These chapters also begin to develop the So What, or the implications, for our classrooms.

Part III takes the more general implications described in the first two parts and begins to flesh them out for the reader. More detail and specificity are warranted and will give a roadmap to professors by helping them determine how best to reach their students. The first half of Part III is truly the *implications* part or more of the So What. More succinctly, this art helps to answer the question, "What are the implications for my own teaching?"

For example, in his book, *What the Best Professors Do*, Ken Bain focuses his research on "four fundamental inquiries":

1. What should my students be able to do intellectually, physically, or emotionally as a result of their learning?
2. How can I best help and encourage them to develop those abilities and the habits of the heart and mind to use them?
3. How can my students and I best understand the nature, quality, and progress of their learning? And
4. How can I evaluate my efforts to foster that learning?[14]

Robert Leamnson warns, "During the grandest disquisition, what goes on in the heads of students is not comparable to what goes on in the head of the speaker. That fact has enormous import for the development of good pedagogy."[15] Further, we know that instructor control of motivation—external motivation, if you will—can negatively impact internal motivation of the learner—the student will not take ownership for their learning, rather they will seek the external reward instead.

The National Research Council commissioned a study to explore "the critical issue of how better to link the findings of research on the science of learning to actual practice in the classroom."[16] In this research, John Bransford and his colleagues warn us that we have begun to focus on breadth as opposed to depth in our curriculum. It's the notorious paradox of the curriculum that is a mile wide and an inch deep. The worry is that we spend our time briefly covering everything and never focusing on anything.

Bransford's group went further in their analysis. Many designs for curriculum, instruction, and assessment practices fail to emphasize the importance of conditionalized knowledge. For example, texts often present facts and formulas with little attention to helping students learn the conditions under which they are most useful. Many assessments measure only propositional (factual) knowledge and never ask whether students know when, where, and why to use that knowledge.[17]

Richard Resnick's work is cited by Bransford's committee: "A third contrast between schools and everyday environments is that abstract reasoning is often emphasized in school, whereas contextualized reasoning is often used in everyday settings. Reasoning can be improved when abstract logical arguments are embedded in concrete contexts."[18] More particularly with respect to adult learners, Laurie Materna explains:

> Having a more extensive base of previous life experiences yields new associations to link with new learning opportunities. Adults are by far more self-directed and autonomous learners than their younger counterparts. They seek out relevant information to expand their knowledge base in order to improve productivity at work and quality in living. Brain-compatible learning strategies offer adults the opportunity to concepts directly and to modify the application to fit their needs.[19]

Further, we know that the brain does not commit to memory a precise duplicate of what it experienced or read—there simply is not the available space or energy in the brain to accomplish this. After all, the brain uses about the same amount of energy as a twenty-watt lightbulb. What the brain does rather than creating a precise memory is to replicate a generalized version across various regions of the brain. This is an efficient method that is prone to error, however. Another problem with this process is that incorrect comprehension or original misinformation can remain encoded throughout the brain,[20] referred to as the "continued influence effect."[21] Such memories are quite difficult to change and need purposeful mitigation strategies to correct.

The final portion of Part III is devoted to *application*. This part can be viewed as the "hands-on" part, or more of the Now What. Using the three main theories of learning as foundational launching pads for how to approach a higher education curriculum and instructional processes, curriculum maps, methods of teaching, sample assignments, and sample assessments are supplied to offer a concrete representation of what brain theory looks like in the classroom. In other words, as a professor, Now What are the applications to my own classroom and teaching?

We will show that how we try to reach our students might change. Ken Bain explains: "At the core of most professors' ideas about teaching is a focus on what the teacher does rather than on what the students are supposed to learn. . . . In contrast, the best educators thought of teaching as anything they might do to help and encourage students to learn. Teaching is engaging students, engineering an environment in which they learn."[22]

Employers often expect different attributes in their employees than those we prepare. According to Bransford and his colleagues, "Society envisions graduates of school systems who can identify and solve problems and can make contributions to society throughout their lifetime—who display the qualities of 'adaptive expertise.' . . . To achieve this vision requires rethinking what is taught, how teachers teach, and how what students learn is assessed."[23]

The actual practice of real authentic learning takes time and practice. The type of learning and teaching we are suggesting takes a great deal of time for both the students and the teachers. In a concluding statement to her book, Jane Healy expresses: "Learning is something that [students] do, not something that is done to them. You have the wisdom to guide the process but not the power to control it. Listen, watch, have patience, enjoy the journey—and the product will take care of itself."[24]

NOTES

1. Erin Hastings and Robin West, "Goal Orientation and Self-Efficacy in Relation to Memory in Adulthood," *Aging, Neuropsychology, and Cognition* 18, no. 4 (2011): 471–93, https://doi.org/10.1080/13825585.2011.575926.

2. Benjamin Bloom, M. Engelhart, E. Furst, Hill, and W. Krathwohl, Taxonomy of Educational Objectives: The Classification of Educational Goals (New York: David McKay Company, 1956).

3. Lorin Anderson and David Krathwohl, eds., *A Taxonomy for Learning, Teaching, and Assessing: A Revision of Bloom's Taxonomy of Educational Objectives* (New York: Longman, 2001). Anderson and Krathwohl (one of the original authors) reframed the original taxonomy from using nouns to describe the levels of objectives to verb or action-oriented descriptors. They also changed the top levels, now considering "create" as a higher-order outcome over "evaluate."

4. Robert Marzano and John Kendall, *The New Taxonomy of Educational Objectives* (Thousand Oaks, CA: Corwin Press, 2006). And Grant Wiggins and J. McTighe, *Understanding by Design* (Alexandria, VA: Association for Supervision and Curriculum Development, 2005). Other versions have been created, as well, but the work of Anderson and Marzano is the most often cited in educational circles. Debate continues whether the taxonomy truly is a hierarchy or simply a series of different types of learning objectives each independent of one another and of no less or more importance than the others, but simply stating the type. For the sake of this book, the differentiation is more academic and not so relevant. Other derivative versions include affective and psychomotor domains (even Bloom created taxonomies for these domains), and cognitive and mental processes, for example.

5. Eric Jensen and Liesl McConchie, *Brain-Based Learning: Teaching the Way Students Really Learn* (Thousand Oaks, CA: Corwin Press, 2020), 2. Jensen and McConchie add: "The brain does not learn on demand according to a school's rigid, inflexible schedule" (2).

6. Richard Restak, *The New Brain: How the Modern Age is Rewiring Your Brain* (Emmaus, Pennsylvania: Rodale Press, 2003), 32.

7. Laurie Materna, *Jump Start the Adult Learner: How to Engage and Motivate Adults Using Brain-Compatible Strategies* (Thousand Oaks, CA: Corwin Press, 2007), xii.

8. Robert Sylwester, *A Celebration of Neurons: An Educator's Guide to the Human Brain* (Alexandria, VA: Association for Supervision and Curriculum Development, 1995), 116.

9. Michio Kaku, *The Future of the Mind: The Scientific Quest to Understand, Enhance, and Empower the Mind* (New York: Doubleday, 2014).

10. National Academies, *How People Learn II*, 70.

How do people orchestrate their own learning? Three key ways are through metacognition, executive function, and self-regulation. *Metacognition* is the ability to monitor and regulate one's own cognitive processes and to consciously regulate behavior, including affective behavior. . . . [*E*]*xecutive function*, refers to cognitive and neural processing that involves the overall regulation of thinking and behavior and the higher-order processes that enable people to plan, sequence, initiate, and sustain their behavior toward some goal, incorporating feedback and making adjustments. *Self-regulation* refers to learning that is focused by means of metacognition, strategic action, and motivation to learn. The integration and interrelation of these dimensions of processing is also critical for deeper or higher-order learning, and for the development of complex skills and knowledge such as reasoning, problem solving, and critical thinking.

11. Ken Bain, *What the Best College Teachers Do* (Cambridge, MA: Harvard University Press, 2004), 33.

12. Materna, *Jump Start the Adult Learner*, 25.

13. National Academies, *How People Learn II*, 2.

14. Bain, *What the Best College Teachers Do*, 49.

15. Robert Leamnson, *Thinking about Teaching and Learning: Developing Habits of Learning with First Year College and University Students* (Sterling, VA: Sylus Publishing, 1999), 17.

16. John Bransford, Ann Brown, and Rodney Cocking, eds., *How People Learn: Brain, Mind, Experience, and School* (Washington, DC: National Academy Press, 2000), vii.

17. Bransford et al., *How People Learn*, 49.

18. Bransford et al., *How People Learn*, 74.

19. Materna, *Jump Start the Adult Learner*, 41.

20. K. H. Ecker Ullrich, Briony Swire, and Stephan Lewandowsky, "Correcting Misinformation—A Challenge for Education and Cognitive Science," in *Processing Inaccurate Information: Theoretical and Implied Perspectives from Cognitive Science and the Educational Sciences*, edited by David Rapp and Jason Braasch (Cambridge, MA: MIT Press, 2014), 15.

21. Colleen Seifert, "The Continued Influence Effect: The Persistence of Misinformation in Memory and Reasoning Following Correction," in *Processing Inaccurate Information: Theoretical and Implied Perspectives from Cognitive Science and the Educational Sciences*, edited by David Rapp and Jason Braasch (Cambridge, MA: MIT Press, 2014), 39.

22. Bain, *What the Best College Teachers Do*, 48–49.

23. Bransford et al., *How People Learn*, 133.

24. Jane Healy, *Your Child's Growing Mind: Brain Development and Learning from Birth to Adolescence* (New York: Broadway Books, 2007), 304.

Part I

The Brain

Remarkable insights into our understanding of the human brain have been made in recent years. This research has led to prescient findings that impact how students learn, how we teach them, and how we assess their learning and the effectiveness of our teaching. We have found that the intuitions and practices of the best experienced professors are supported by these insights with respect to the science and the art of teaching.

Early pronouncements of isolated portions of the brain being solely responsible for learning and memory were spurious. We have come to understand that while various regions of the brain maintain some primacy for different aspects of thinking, learning, and memory, none of this takes place in isolation.[1] Even more, the brain doesn't think and learn in isolation from the rest of the body. All of this work is part of a complex, dynamic, and even, at times, error-prone set of integrated systems. It is from this perspective that we begin our journey into the brain before we move into the more granular aspects of the human mind and how it thinks and learns.

NATURE AND NURTURE

This age-old debate has pitted educators against one another from time immemorial. Is it nature or nurture that impacts student learning the most? Brain researchers and cognitive scientists have settled the debate. It's not either/or; it's both/and. They are emphatic about this point. Both our genetic makeup and our environment play critical interconnected roles in our development. It is nonsensical to talk of one without the other. It comes down to what we do with what we have been given.[2]

Educational psychologist Jane Healy explains: "There is such a constant interaction between basic capacity and experience from the moment of a baby's conception that the question is impossible to answer—and really unnecessary—to answer."[3] Moreover, biology, relationships, social experiences, and culture all play essential roles in brain development.[4]

We do know the human brain is born ready to learn and adapt to do almost anything. It can learn to be fluent in any language and to master untold skills in virtually any field. The neurons and supporting glial cells are there from birth; they just need to make the connections through processes of learning and experiences. A child's brain increases in size by four by the time they reach school age and is 90 percent of the adult brain in volume by that time.[5]

Former professor at the University of Oregon Robert Sylwester wrote *A Celebration of Neurons* for the Association of Supervision and Curriculum Development. This seminal work explains not only brain development but application to the classroom, as well. He writes, in part:

Although most of a brain's lifetime supply of neurons are in place shortly after birth, many of the axon-dendrite connections that process cognitive information develop after birth, as a brain gradually adapts to its environment and makes itself the unique result of its own experience. In the human brain, this post birth development results in a weight increase from about one pound at birth, to two pounds at age one, to three pounds at late adolescent maturation.[6]

Various portions of the brain grow, develop, and mature at different rates and at different stages. These will be discussed in the pages to come. For now, it is important to understand that many of our college students have brains that are continuing to physically grow and develop, and certain higher cognitive functions have yet to fully mature.

Often times we hear how the brain functions and processes information like a computer. Such reasoning is not only faulty but it leads to poor strategies for teaching. Rather, the human brain grows and functions much more organically and dynamically—a jungle or ecological metaphor, if you will. Neural connections grow while others die off. Connections are intricately woven throughout the brain and across systems. Different portions of the brain work together in a symbiotic process creating memories and new learning.

As such, this natural understanding of the brain explains its predominate and immediate purpose: survival. It is born to survive, to perceive threats, and subsequently to determine the best course of action. If a threat is sensed, the brain goes into survival mode—fight or flight, if you will—and no higher-order functioning or thinking will take place. Thus, implications of intimidating or stress-filled classrooms and exams are profound.

THE UNIFIED WHOLE

In order to survive, the brain system is intricately interconnected with other body systems. Professors Eric Jensen and Liesl McConchie note: "Most every process runs through multiple systems (sympathetic, digestive, immune, etc.) and engages not one, but multiple structures (prefrontal cortex, hypothalamus, amygdala, etc.) in the brain and body."[7] Robert Sylwester adds the endocrine and circulatory systems to this mix. "Our circulatory system transports each blood cell or hormone molecule to any of numerous sites in our body prepared to receive it. It's a simple system that creates a whole body/brain response to a whole body/brain problem."[8] To punctuate the point, Sylwester concludes:

> Our brain, endocrine, and immune systems, long viewed as separate entities, are now seen as an integrated biochemical system. Our emotional system is located principally in our brain, immune, and endocrine systems, but it also affects such organs as our heart, lungs, stomach, and skin.[9]

Not only should we think of the body/brain as a singular unified system but the brain itself must be considered a singular whole with no part operating by itself.[10] "The brain's functioning is so complex that multiple areas and systems of neural connections must work together for any task. For example, brain scans of adults doing related language activities—listening, reading out loud, reading silently, and thinking up words—show activity scattered all over the brain," according to Dr. Jane Healy.[11]

Awareness, attention, memory, and thinking are distributed throughout the brain. Not any one area is solely responsible for any of these aspects. Again, Healy explains: "Human memory depends upon widespread circuits and chemical interactions as well as specialized areas."[12] Robert Sylwester continues: "Thought emerges out of attention when a continuous, quite active, synchronized firing pattern resonates between a critical mass of related neural networks in the thalamus (which processes the immediate situation) and the cortex (which contains memories related to objects and events in the immediate situation)."[13]

The hippocampus directs memories to different parts of the brain. Kaku explained that "long-term memories are encoded not electronically, but at the level of protein molecules."[14] Hence, memory reconstruction is a process of encoding and storing experiences in the brain. The encoded memory is not an exact duplicate of the experience. Rather, it is a subjective representation.[15] Memories are malleable as they are stored across various regions of the brain. As other representative memories are stored in these regions, the memories may become commingled, blurred, and edited. As such, professors need to routinely check for students' understanding and misunderstanding.

Eminent psychologist and author of *Finding Flow*, Mihalyi Csikszentmihalyi, writes, "Emotions, intentions, and thoughts do not pass through consciousness as separate strands of experience, but that they are constantly interconnected, and modify each other as they go along."[16] Describing, for example, the complexity of learning and playing music, Daniel Levitin notes:

> At a neural level, playing an instrument requires the orchestration of regions in our primitive, reptilian brain—the cerebellum and the brain stem—as well as higher cognitive systems such as the motor cortex (in the parietal lobe) and the planning regions of our frontal lobes, the most advanced region of the brain.[17]

Perhaps the most comprehensive description of the regions of the human brain, the various parts and their unique primacy with respect to education, as well as the intricacies of their interactions with one another is provided by former nursing professor Laurie Materna. She describes the three primary regions of the brain including the lower, middle, and upper regions.[18] The first is the more primitive brain stem that sits atop the spinal column. This leads to the surrounding middle brain and then ultimately to the upper and outer brain. (See the note 18 and later in Part I for greater detail).

The lower brain is the first to develop—out of necessity—for this is the region responsible for our survival. It is the middle and upper regions that take longer to mature and much longer to develop intellectually. Some of the higher functioning areas won't develop until adolescence and even young adulthood. These are the students in your classrooms—those whose higher-level thinking is still maturing. The frontal lobes, the executive control center of the brain, may not fully mature for thirty years!

If the brain—the lower brain—senses the person may be in danger, the whole body goes into survival mode and higher-order thinking will not occur. If the student feels they will be embarrassed or humiliated, they will focus their attention on "saving face," or getting out of the classroom or awkward situation, certainly not on the learning objective for the day. Should the student feel their emotional or mental survival is not an issue, the middle brain or the limbic system becomes activated.

These portions of the brain devoted to producing emotions help long-term memories take root. It is at these two lower regions of the brain that the individual determines the relevancy of what is to be learned. If the concept is found to be relevant, it will likely be stored in short-term working memory and perhaps then on to long-term memory. Then the neocortex of the upper and outer layer of the brain, responsible for higher-level thinking, is activated. In this way, the whole brain continues to work together with stored long-term memories in both the emotional portions of the brain and with the thinking regions of the brain.

Emotions are critical according to brain research and to learning theory. If the learning environment is positive, the brain will more likely focus on the teaching objective and instigate higher-level thinking. If, on the other hand, the learning environment is negative, the brain will downshift into survival mode and limit thinking. As such, emotion is the trigger point to what comes next. Relevance and an emotionally supportive environment lay the foundation for learning.

As has been discussed, learning and thinking are not isolated endeavors to particular parts of the brain. The entire brain is involved in all cognition even though certain areas may have primacy over others for certain aspects. We're fortunate this is the case, for in instances of traumatic injury to a certain region of the brain, other regions can still carry on because of their memories and associated abilities. This inherent redundancy in brain functioning and the brain's plasticity are crucial to our survival.

Cognition and memories are strengthened, as a matter of fact, by rich experiences and by activating multiple regions of the brain using the different senses. The more senses involved and the more experiences we have, the greater the ability to remember and to think at higher levels. Most learners (40–65 percent) would be considered visual learners, according to Colin Rose. Auditory learners comprise another 25 to 30 percent, and 5 to 15 percent are primarily kinesthetic learners.[19] Think of the implications for your classroom.

The chart below (Figure 1.1) shows various parts of the cortex and their primacy in various learning modalities.

Now let us turn our attention to a more granular description of the various regions and subregions of the human brain—to learn their primary roles and how they interact with one another. Then we can focus on how our students' brains grow and develop before we move to implications for our own teaching and assessment strategies.

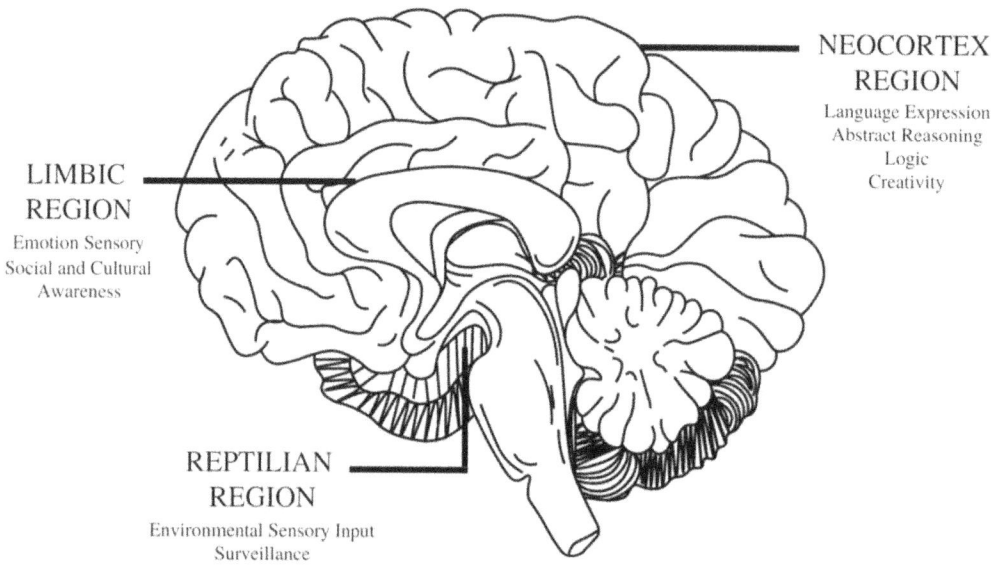

Figure 1.1. Brain Regions Where Learning Takes Place
Source: Created by Dr. Toni Bailey.

NEURONS

The most fundamental units of our brain are the cells. The brain is made up of two primary types of cells—the neurons and the glial cells. We consider the neurons as the thinking cells associated with the brain, while the glial cells are the support cells to the neurons.

Glial cells far outnumber the neurons that they support. Our brains have trillions of glial cells that provide nutrition to the neurons, help to repair the neurons, and protect the neurons from harmful bacteria. Glial cells also produce the protein myelin that coats and protects neurons as they become more active. The myelin coating, or sheath, further helps the neurons to fire more quickly and efficiently. It has been reported that Albert Einstein's brain had a larger number of glial cells compared to the average person.[20]

A child is born with virtually all the neurons they will ever need, estimated between 100 billion or even up to 1 trillion. That is the nature; the rest is the nurture. A child's brain is born with the ability to learn any language fluently, to learn any musical instrument, to acquire thinking skills for any task that they are given. The neurons are there from the beginning.

What the newborn brain cells do not have are the enormous array of interconnections with other neurons and other regions of the brain that an adult brain has acquired through experience—through learning. The brain can make adjustments and learn because of its immense capability to adapt and to make new connections—a term called "plasticity"—a process that can last a lifetime.

The neuron is an amazing cell. (See Figure 1.2 for detail about neurons and how they connect). We are born with virtually all the neurons we will ever need. The more a neuron is stimulated through use—experience or learning, if you will—the stronger it becomes. It doesn't become stronger by itself in isolation, however; it becomes stronger with its interconnections with other neurons and nerves. The process of connecting to other neurons is called neural branching. Neurons can connect to thousands of other neurons. Cells that are not used or activated through stimulation become weaker and eventually wither away—a process called neural pruning.

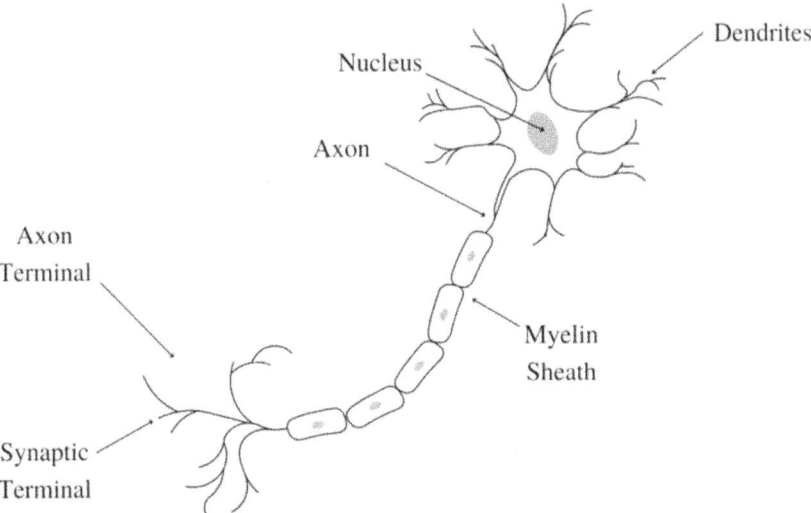

Figure 1.2. Diagram of a Neuron
Source: Created by Dr. Toni Bailey.

"Neural networks are collections of neurons that constantly rewire and reinforce themselves after learning a new task," according to Michio Kaku in *The Future of the Mind*.[21] He goes on to add, "Neural networks are parallel, with one hundred billion neurons firing at the same time in order to accomplish one goal: to learn."

Indeed, the difference between an infant's brain and an adult's brain is not the number of neurons so much as the number of connections or synapses. As such, the infant's brain weighs approximately one pound and doubles in weight during the first year. By the time the child reaches young adulthood their brain has reached three pounds. Even the very act of thinking causes the neurons to fire and to strengthen, just as it does with physical sensing or activity.

As can be seen from figure 1.2, each neuron has a cell body with dendrite spines on one end. These dendrites receive chemical signals, or neurotransmitters,[22] from other cells. The cell body turns the chemical signal into an electrical impulse that travels down the cell's axon (up to a meter in length or more) where it gets turned back into a chemical at the synaptic junction between the neuron and thousands of other neurons in its region. No neuron directly touches another; rather, they are awash in a chemical bath with other neurons—sending and receiving, stimulating or inhibiting, further action. The process of thinking causes cells to communicate, as described by Professor Laurie Materna:

> Each time the brain thinks a thought, these connections are fired up, modifying the electrochemical wiring. The more novel and stimulating the thought is, the more likely it will activate a new connection . . . [which] trigger the electrochemical process that promotes long-term memory.[23]

Thinking and memories are created when groups or networks of neurons fire across regions of the brain. No area is solely responsible for a particular thought or memory. Each network is responsible for a portion of the thinking or memory, but together they complete the whole picture. Likewise, people's memories are not exact copies of an event. Rather, they are an approximate reconstruction and are thus prone to error.[24]

Sylwester adds, "Thought emerges out of attention when a continuous, quite active, synchronized firing pattern resonates between a critical mass of related neural networks in the thalamus (which processes the immediate situation) and the cortex (which contains memories)."[25] Each neuron is part of the entire thought or memory. The more often these neurons fire with additional thinking or experiences, the stronger they become and the easier it becomes for them to be reactivated—they become more efficient.

Thus, in the words of Dr. Richard Restak, "Intelligence is plastic and modifiable. All of our experiences result in the formation of neuronal circuits. The richer, more varied, and more challenging the experiences, the more elaborate the neuronal circuits."[26] This learning is caused by the brain purposefully weaving together past experiences within the current context.

How are such tiny neurons able to interact in such complex ways across various regions of the brains instantaneously? Recent scientific breakthroughs provide answers. Cognitive scientist and philosophy professor at the University of British Columbia Evan Thompson explains in part that the brain produces electromagnetic fields (or neuroelectric fields).

> When many neurons are interconnected to formal neural networks, the sum or superposition of their electrical fields generates macroscopic neuroelectrical fields at a higher level of complexity. . . . Collectively, however, neurons synchronize their action potentials, both locally and across large distances, and this temporal synchronization of an enormous number of action potentials produces the coherent and large-scale electrodynamical states of the brain that correlate with various modes of consciousness.[27]

Further, some researchers have concluded that neural synapses communicate in quantum wave patterns enabling communication to occur throughout the brain in an instant in incalculable ways. Michael Talbot has gone as far as to consider the human brain a model of holographic thinking. Citing the work of Austrian neuroscientist Karl Pribram, Talbot recognizes each neuron as holding a partial piece of a thought's or a memory's full picture, but through complex interference patterns in the synapses, a full holographic image emerges.[28]

Neurons and glial cells are the most fundamental units found throughout every region of the brain. It is now time to discuss the various regions from the most primitive portion (the brain stem) to the most advanced region (the cortex)—the part that makes us uniquely human and capable of intricate, creative, and elaborate thinking.

BRAIN GROWTH AND DEVELOPMENT

The human brain, like that of animals, is primed foremost for survival. Humans, however, have advanced brains that are capable of great learning, creativity, and cognition. Such great abilities take time to develop after survival is ensured. Robert Sylwester explaines it this way:

> The basic genetic developmental pattern for our brain is thus quite simple and straightforward: (1) create an initial excess of cells and connections among related areas—in effect, temporarily wire up everything to everything, (2) use emotion, experience, and learning to strengthen the useful connections, and then prune away the unused and inefficient, and (3) maintain enough synaptic flexibility (commonly called *plasticity*) to allow neural network connections to shift about throughout life as conditions change and new problem-solving challenges emerge.[29]

As has been noted earlier, one way to think of the brain is with it encapsulating three main sections—a triune brain, if you will: the lower brain (the survival brain), the middle brain (the brain associated with emotion and working memory), and the upper brain (the brain regions devoted to rational, creative, long-term memory, and higher-order thinking). These areas will be described in greater detail later in this part.

Different regions of the brain, just as the rest of the human body, mature and develop at different rates and at different critical times. Often, parents worry that their child is not making cognitive gains at the same time or pace their peers might be. Most likely the child is making physical gains in other parts of their body—motor development, for example, instead. Or portions of their brain are developing that cannot be as easily observed. In either case, a child's brain and body are always developing on their own timetable, and it is best not to rush it but, rather, to be prepared when it is ready. In other words, it is unnecessary and perhaps counterproductive to worry and to force learning when the child's brain is not developmentally ready.

Because it is devoted to our survival, the lower brain is virtually primed at birth to function immediately and to respond to the environment. It takes in sensory inputs to determine whether a flight or fight response is warranted, or if further processing by the middle brain is appropriate. As such, the middle brain takes longer to mature, and even its different regions develop at different rates.

The most advanced portions of the brain, those in the upper brain, take the longest to mature and develop, often times into adulthood, and are ever adapting or learning. Educational psychology professors Jeanne Ellis Ormrod and Brett Jones stipulate, "The prefrontal cortex—the part of the brain responsible for planning, decision making, and many other advanced reasoning processes—is especially slow to mature and doesn't take on a truly adultlike form until individuals reach their early 20s."[30]

It is the prefrontal cortex (or the executive center of the brain) that is associated with reasoning, long-term memory, self-control, attention, planning, and judgment and is the last area of the brain to mature.[31] The frontal lobes prune neurons that an individual's experience shows to be irrelevant or unnecessary. This is also the critical time when myelination is making its greatest impact on the cortex. The implications of this knowledge have great import for college professors, as we will see later in subsequent pages.

The process of learning actually makes physical and structural changes to the brain. Learning creates more synapses, strengthens the neurons and connections that already exist making them more efficient, and the cortex actually gains in weight the more it is used. And not only does the brain modify itself through its plasticity, but it builds in redundancy and distributes learning across various regions of the brain. "To continue to function after a brain injury requires that a blow to a single part of the brain doesn't shut down the whole system. Important brain systems evolved additional, supplementary pathways," according to neuroscientist Daniel Levitin.[32]

All of learning is interconnected throughout the brain. We know memories and thinking don't reside in only particular regions of the brain, but these various parts impact the complete learning experience. Further, these brain regions affect various systems throughout the entire body. For example, according to Sylwester,

> The principal brain mechanisms involved in procedural memories are the amygdala (our brain's emotional center located in the limbic system), the cerebellum (located in the lower back of the brain), and the autonomic nervous system (which regulates circulation and respiration)—but procedural memories also involve altered muscle systems.[33]

So, even the very act of thinking impacts the brain itself—it strengthens neurons, creates additional synapses, and furthers interconnectivity throughout the brain, indeed, throughout the body. Even dreams activate the same neurons and regions of the brain as do waking experiences and thinking.[34]

REGIONS OF THE BRAIN

As previously noted, there are three primary levels of the human brain: lower, middle, and upper. Each has increasing complexity, takes longer to develop and mature, and plays escalating roles in our intelligence. We'll start with a brief overview of the most basic and primitive portion of the human brain: the lower brain.[35]

The lower brain consists of the brain stem and the cerebellum. The brain stem sits atop of the spinal cord and is the terminus of all the senses, with the exception of smell. It regulates our body's functions of respiration and blood circulation. It is the brain stem that has primary responsibility to sense danger. If it does sense danger, it automatically decides on a path for fight or flight, or perhaps even freeze. As such, further advanced cognition does not take place, unless the person purposefully and rationally considers the circumstances to determine whether or not other options are better. A student who feels threatened in the classroom likely will focus more on survival—saving face—than on the lesson's objective for the day—it is only natural they do so.

The cerebellum is the other portion of the lower brain and is responsible for physical movement and kinesthetic memories. This region of the brain has more neurons than the rest of the brain regions combined, and it connects with all regions at the same time. Thus, it plays a central role in coordinating thoughts and memories and processing information, including our most high-level cognition. Further, the cerebellum helps us operate at a subconscious level—on autopilot—if you will. Such activities as walking and dreaming, for example, operate here.

Materna explains: "Procedural memories (muscle memory) are accessed through the cerebellum . . . and are best recalled unconsciously."[36] Procedural memories are not limited to this region of the brain, as noted earlier, however. The cerebellum is interconnected with all areas of the brain. In this way, the cerebellum works in tandem with the brain stem's circulation and respiratory systems, and the limbic system (the emotional region of the middle brain) for procedural memories. Because of its integral role in thinking and its central role in physical behavior, implications for teaching are profound and will be discussed in greater detail later in this part and in Part III.

The middle brain is more advanced and takes longer to develop than the lower brain. It is known as the limbic system, encases the brainstem and cerebellum, and contains the thalamus (senses), hippocampus (memories), and amygdala (emotions). The middle brain is responsible for our hormonal and immune systems and for regulating emotions. As such, it connects with our prefrontal cortex as a system check to determine the best response to a given emotional scenario and ties memories to emotions. The limbic system urges action, while the prefrontal cortex urges restraint. While the limbic system sits atop the brain stem and cerebellum, it is surrounded by the neocortex. It is the neocortex that operates at the conscious level, the limbic system works at the unconscious level.

For educators, the limbic system plays a critical role for intrapersonal intelligence. Robert Sylwester explains that this doesn't fully occur until adulthood or late adolescence when the frontal lobes and the prefrontal cortex have matured. Physically, the brain naturally has an emotional response to an input *before* the rational portions of the brain have a chance to respond. As such, it takes conscientious effort to control one's emotions by allowing the executive center of the brain to take the lead.[37]

The thalamus is the processing point for all our senses except smell. "It helps to initiate consciousness and make preliminary classifications of external information," according to Fred Alan Wolf.[38] This organ then further processes incoming information on to the thinking portions of our brain—the cortex—for a more detailed analysis, and it serves as the holding area for short-term memory and attention. It also sends information to the amygdala to determine whether a self-defense posture is necessitated. In this sense, it communicates with the rest of the brain about the outside world. The related hypothalamus regulates important molecules in between our endocrine and nervous systems.

"The hippocampus is responsible for making meaning out of stored memories and converting information from working memory to long-term memory," according to Materna.[39] Like the thalamus, the hippocampus also works directly with the brain's cortex and is important for the learning of facts and rules.[40] In an interesting aside, the wishbone-shaped hippocampus (one located in each hemisphere) is one of the few areas of the brain that can generate new neurons, or the process known as neurogenesis. According to Ormrod and Jones, "The hippocampus also seems to be a central figure in learning, in that it pulls together information it simultaneously receives from various parts of the brain."[41]

The amygdala—again, one in each hemisphere—plays a key role in processing emotions, especially negative emotions such as fear. According to Jensen and McConchie, "The amygdala's primary task is to ensure our survival."[42] It also works directly with the brain's higher-level cortex. It is responsible for long-term memories associated with emotions. In so doing, when a long-term memory is accessed, the amygdala brings along the emotion associated with that memory. It sends its signals on to the hippocampus.

When any of these middle brain regions (thalamus, hippocampus, amygdala) are activated, they send out a combination of neurotransmitters and hormones. This, in part, is one of the reasons emotions play such a critical role in learning and memories. As always, the implications for college professors are incredible and should not go underappreciated. Using emotions positively can help retrieve and strengthen memories and recall as well as automatically activate advanced regions of the brain. It is important to note that too much stress, especially negative stress, can actually cause the hippocampus to shrink. The best educators try to create a classroom environment and curriculum of high challenge but low stress.

The upper brain is what most people think about when we consider education. This region, the cerebrum, contains 85 percent of the brain's mass and takes the longest to develop and mature (into our twenties) and is often what we refer to as gray matter. It contains the two complementary hemispheres, connected by the corpus callosum, and is divided into four lobes: frontal, temporal, parietal, and occipital. The cerebrum is wrapped by a thin layer—six layers of neurons—known as the neocortex—which we consider the thinking part of the brain. According to Ormrod and Jones:

> Complex thinking, learning, and knowledge are located primarily in the upper and outer parts of the brain collectively known as the cortex. . . . The portion of the cortex located near the forehead, known as the prefrontal cortex, is largely responsible for a wide variety of distinctly human activities, including sustained attention, reasoning, planning, decision making, coordinating complex activities, and preventing nonproductive thoughts and behaviors.[43]

It is in this portion of the brain where complex thinking takes place. Here we find the processes of problem-solving, creativity, analysis, synthesis, and evaluation—the higher levels on Bloom's Taxonomy.[44] While the limbic system is often referred to as the brain's inner shell, the cortex can be referred to as its outer shell. Further, while the limbic system is better known for concerning itself with negative emotions and fight or flight responses, the prefrontal cortex regulates such emotions as empathy, compassion, and altruism.[45] Interestingly, Andrew Holecek explains:

> The prefrontal cortex is deactivated when we sleep. This part of the brain is involved with "executive function," which relates to the ability to determine good and bad, to differentiate between conflicting thoughts, to predict outcomes, to apply moral values, and to moderate social behavior . . . the prefrontal cortex isn't fully developed until age twenty-five, which leads to bad decisions and poor social control. Executive function is "parental" function.[46]

Neurons in the cortex are bundled together into narrow strands each of which is responsible for specific functions or sensory information. They interconnect with one another, both vertically and horizontally, and come together to paint a clear picture or interpretation of the information being processed.[47] For example, one bundle may be responsible for interpreting a particular sound, while others are responsible for other individual sounds. When intertwined together, they understand a complete piece of music. Couple this neural collection with other neural columns interpreting various visual and other sensory inputs, previous knowledge, memories, and emotions, a staggering and dynamic interplay of neural network activity comes together for a complete experience.

The cerebrum, as noted, is divided into four lobes in each hemisphere. The frontal lobes are located behind the forehead. They consist of the motor cortex and the prefrontal cortex. The former coordinates our physical activity. The prefrontal cortex is responsible for higher-level thinking, planning, and abstract reasoning, in particular. It controls our conscious behavior and integrates working memory. Importantly, our frontal lobes help to regulate our emotions and judgments and can keep us from overreacting to emotionally charged situations. This is the executive control center of our brain; it's the region that matures last and is the region we need to teach students how to use to make wise decisions.

The temporal lobes are located above each ear and are responsible for hearing, memory, and meaning-making. These lobes also play a role in language. The parietal lobes, which are located across the top of the cerebrum, are responsible for sensory processing such as touch and spatial understanding. They also play a primary role in language processing. Across the back of the head are the occipital lobes, which process visual information.

While each regional lobe has primary areas of responsibility associated with it, when each is activated, the other regions are activated as well in a highly orchestrated fashion—they do not work in isolation from one another. Together, they recognize and create patterns and meaning and knowledge. They retrieve experiences from memory and create new memories. Up to 99 percent of this activity is unconscious. According to Materna: "Implications for education are profound: Learners are unconsciously absorbing, interpreting, and acting upon environmental cues over and above the actual lesson presented to their conscious minds."[48]

On a related topic, Douglas Hacker expresses that under normal conditions people overlook errors 40 percent of the time in their text reading.[49] Most likely they lose focus or are rushed for time. They may overlook misinformation in the writing or not fully comprehend what they have simply scanned. Again, the implications are breathtaking. Student reading needs to be purposeful, focused, and deliberate. Approaches need to be used to check student understanding before incorrect learning is transferred into long-term memory.

Once correct or incorrect information is processed or encoded in the brain, it is there. It cannot simply be erased like a computer model. Even more, the information or memory is not simply located in one place—it's diffused across the brain. So, learning is robust, but so is incorrect learning. It is difficult to relearn something correctly once learned incorrectly. It takes deliberative effort and time to compensate or correct.

A great deal has been made about the brain's two hemispheres and how we identify ourselves as either right-brained or left-brained. Much of this discussion has been overblown, yet differences between the cerebral hemispheres do exist. The two distinct halves, or lobes, are connected by a thick band of millions of fibrous neural cells known as the corpus callosum. The corpus callosum is the pathway for communication and collaboration between the two hemispheres. It is critical for the two hemispheres to have their efforts coordinated through the corpus callosum. In the words of Robert Sylwester:

> The left hemisphere (in most people) processes the objective content of language—*what* was said—while the right hemisphere processes the emotional content of facial expressions, gestures, and language intonation—*how* it was said. By processing related information from different perspectives, the hemispheres collaborate to produce something that becomes a unified mental experience.[50]

Lateralization among the two hemispheres does exist. Language, speech, and logical thinking primarily take place in the left hemisphere, while the right hemisphere plays a more dominate role in visual and spatial tasks.[51] The lobe sizes differ in the two hemispheres. For example, the right frontal lobe is larger than its counterpart, while the left occipital lobe is larger than the right. In addition, the left hemisphere contains more dopamine, while the right half contains more norepinephrine.[52]

Michio Kaku explains, "The left brain is the dominant one and makes the final decisions. Commands pass from the left brain to the right brain via the corpus callosum."[53] The right hemisphere generally sees or synthesizes the whole picture and is intuitive, empathetic, and artistic, while the left is sequential, analytical, mathematical, and detail-oriented. The bottom line, however, is that both hemispheres work together for full understanding—the strengths of both hemispheres must work together for optimal learning to take place.

With a very interesting insight, Andrew Holecek notes that lucid dreams activate the brain in the same way as waking life. If you work on a math problem in your dream, for example, your left hemisphere is stimulated just as it would be during the day. If you sing in your dream, the right hemisphere is activated.[54] Leonard Shlain also notes an intriguing insight: "Each hemisphere of the brain controls the muscles of the body's opposite side, . . . To ensure versatility in case of injury, each hemisphere has some capacity to perform the other side's functions."[55]

The left hemisphere may be more responsible for routine information processing and the right more for novel situations. The left hemisphere is considered more rational, analytical, and logical, while the right hemisphere is more intuitive, integrative, and relational. The left analyzes the details, and the right sees the big picture. If a student reads a passage in the text, their left hemisphere takes primacy. If they encounter a photograph as they read, their right hemisphere may take the lead.[56]

Likewise, when students process language, "the right hemisphere helps with the conceptual understanding, whereas the left is adept with the sequence and the grammar," according to Jane Healy.[57] Both hemispheres work together for a comprehensive understanding. Thus, discussions of right- or left-brained learners is too simplistic.[58] See figure 1.3 for clarity.

Before we turn our attention to general implications for professors, it will be worth a visit to the literature with respect to what we know about how the brains of experts and geniuses work. It has been determined that, organically speaking, experts in some fields have more neurons and neuron connections than nonexperts.[59]

According to John Bransford and his colleagues, experts—because of their extensive knowledge and experience—organize and analyze information differently than most people. These authors note key differences and implications for teaching:

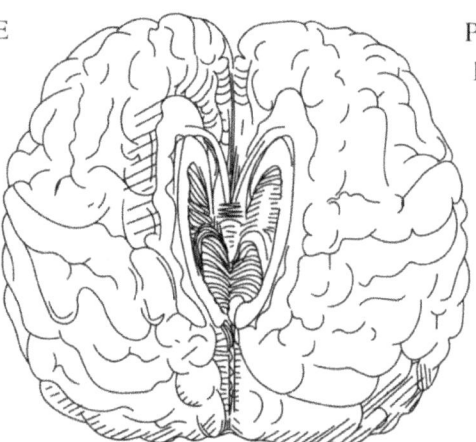

PROCLIVITIES OF THE LEFT HEMISPHERE

Details
Logic
Time-Bound
Language Fundamentals
Fine Motor Skills
Routines
Order
Sensory Processors

PROCLIVITIES OF THE RIGHT HEMISPHERE

The Whole Picture
Intuition
Spatial Awareness
Language Gesture
Hands-On
Creativity
Conceptual Processors
Imagination

Primary Responsibility of Each Hemisphere
Source: Created by Dr. Toni Bailey.

1. Experts notice features and meaningful patterns of information that are not noticed by novices.
2. Experts have acquired a great deal of content knowledge that is organized in ways that reflect a deep understanding of their subject matter.
3. Experts' knowledge cannot be reduced to sets of isolated facts or propositions but, instead, reflects contexts of applicability: that is, the knowledge is "conditionalized" on a set of circumstances.
4. Experts are able to flexibly retrieve important aspects of their knowledge with little attentional effort.
5. Though experts know their disciplines thoroughly, this does not guarantee that they are able to teach others.
6. Experts have varying levels of flexibility in their approach to new situations.[60]

In terms of giftedness, Jane Healy has created her own list of attributes of these students. They:

1. Take more time to think strategically about problems and less time to solve them.
2. Seeks wholes, patterns, and relationships.
3. "Web" knowledge (that is—establish mental categories and connect new ideas to them).
4. Prefer complexity.
5. View learning as an adventure.
6. Possess significant self-discipline to plan and implement projects.[61]

In looking at the brains of musicians, Robert Sylwester explains:

> For most people, music processing is centered in the right hemisphere (though rhythm is one element of music processed in the left hemisphere). . . . Trained musicians often activate left hemisphere mechanisms while listening to music, probably because they are also analyzing the music.[62]

Daniel Levitin explains in greater detail why this may be the case. "Musical training appears to have the effect of shifting some music processing from the right (imagistic) hemisphere to the left (logical) hemisphere, as musicians learn to talk about—and perhaps think about—music using linguistic terms."[63]

Such research gives educators hope that they can help develop latent talent in students, while perhaps not to the level of genius, certainly to the level of expertise or competence. "Following certain brain-based guidelines anyone can achieve expert performance in sports, athletics, and academic pursuits," according to Richard Restak.[64] Restak added to the view that musicians modify their brain organization through focus and repetition—moving the focus from the right to the left hemisphere. Specifically referring to genius, he noted they have a particular internal drive and focus:

> exhibited an intense concentration, leading to heightened awareness of each of the many components of their actions coupled with an ability to adapt in ways that led to higher levels of control. . . . [They have] "a rage to master": the willingness of the genius, prodigy, or superior performer to devote almost all waking hours to mastering his or her chosen field of endeavor.[65]

In his study of chess grand masters, Restak discovered that they are better at accessing long-term memories as they have an extensive repertoire of experiences. This vast experience, coupled with an earnest focus, gives them the ability to "recognize positions and problems and to retrieve the solutions."[66] These grand masters "don't have to think; they are recognizing patterns,"[67] which can be retrieved effortlessly. To which he adds:

> The expert . . . golfer, by mentally attending to extremely subtle aspects of his performance during practice sessions, has successfully transferred this knowledge into working memory within his frontal lobes. Later, when under pressure, his brain concentrates on one or more components of his learned procedural skills. For him, task and not ego remain at the forefront of mental activity.[68]

What we have discovered from how the brain learns, recalls memories, creates, makes decisions, and understands has significant implications for the university classroom. The implications should not only impact the way we teach but also the types of assignments we give, and how we assess how well the students have learned and how effectively we have taught them.

GENETIC INFLUENCES

The field of neuroepigenetics is concerned with the idea of determining to what degree environmental and inherited genes are responsible for various cognitive abilities and functions. There are 20,300 genes in the human genome, and researchers have determined that of these there are nearly 900 genes that contribute to cognition.[69]

How our cognitive genes express themselves depends on both nature and nurture. That is, our genes express themselves in a variety of alleles, because of both inherited DNA and responses to the environment, according to Bueno.[70] Heritability is the term used by geneticists to describe how much of a trait is determined by our genes and how much is determined by environmental influences. For example, if a particular trait is 30 percent dependent upon genetics, it is 70 percent dependent upon the environment.

Research indicates that our environments can influence how our genes express themselves.[71] Our bodies can make "epigenetic modifications" to respond to what is happening in our environment.[72] Traits such as high intelligence, cooperativity, grit, and attention have heritability percentages of 33 percent, 13 percent, 37 percent, and 28 percent, respectively.[73] This concept is significant to educators because it implies that teachers' pedagogical approaches, in many cases, create environmental influences that may cause students' genes to express themselves in either proactive or inactive ways.

IMPLICATIONS FOR PROFESSORS

The implications for the college classroom are profound and should lead to significant changes in our learning environments. Many teaching practices of the best professors have been affirmed, and other new challenges have now become evident. While the first half of Part III provides greater detail of educational implications, and the final half of Part III shares concrete examples of curriculum, assignments, and assessments based on these implications, a general overview highlighting these implications is warranted here.

In order to meet the needs of our society and the demands for today's workforce, educators from institutions of higher learning must take a careful re-examination of their curriculum, their pedagogy, their strategies for assessment, their entire classroom experience, and how they relate to their broader communities.

With the college student brain in mind, professors must understand how the brain learns, accesses memories, creates knowledge, and solves problems. Robert Sylwester explained, "Because neurons thrive only in an environment that stimulates them to receive, store, and transmit information, the challenge to educators is simple: define, create, and maintain an emotionally and intellectually stimulating school environment and curriculum."[74] As most of their learning happens at the subconscious level—the classroom environment is crucial.

It is difficult to separate the implications for curriculum, pedagogy, assessment, and the classroom environment from one another as they are all so intricately interrelated. Discussion of teaching incorporates factions of each of these areas as they meld into one another—much like how the brain itself is organized and learns. What follows, however, is an attempt to differentiate key implications in each of these areas beginning with key points about the learner's brain.

The Brain

We know that throughout a person's life their brain's synapses continue to grow—to make complex connections. This plasticity enables new learning to occur throughout one's lifespan and to overcome previous obstacles. "Lasting brain change occurs when new inputs are perceived as highly relevant or compelling," according to Eric Jensen.[75]

The brain is designed first and foremost for survival—to protect the person. If the brain—the lower brain—senses the person may be in danger, the whole body goes into survival mode and higher-level thinking will not occur. If the student feels they will be embarrassed or humiliated, they will focus their attention on "saving face," or getting out of the classroom, certainly not on the objective for the day. If, on the other hand, the student should feel their survival is not an issue, the middle brain—the limbic system—becomes activated.

It is here where the brain seeks relevance and becomes emotionally involved with the context and integrates with memory. Even here, though, the brain can prevent the student from higher-order thinking. "When the amygdala senses uncertainty in any form—physical, emotional, or even social—it harnesses all the brain's energy to focus on the potential threat. This means any cognitive functioning will be at best impaired, if not temporarily halted. . . . [Some students] get lost in the emotional processing and lose focus on learning," according to Jensen.[76]

The sage professor will ensure an emotionally safe classroom environment and harness the power of emotions. This will allow necessary time for other regions of the brain to become actively involved and to integrate working memory with long-term memory. It is the middle and upper regions of the brain that take longer to mature and much longer to develop. Some of the higher functioning areas won't develop until adolescence and even young adulthood. These are the students in your classrooms—those whose higher-level thinking is still maturing.

The frontal lobes, the executive portion of the brain, may not fully mature for thirty years! The professor's job is to help guide the student's growth and use of the executive center—to help them slow down, be thoughtful in their analysis, and to be purposeful in their decision-making and their responses.[77] Professors need to model and reinforce metacognitive and deliberative problem-solving practices.

The entire brain needs to be engaged, preferably through multiple senses, for optimal student learning. Students need to feel safe and able to take intellectual risks. Their emotions will drive attention as they search for relevance and connections to previous learning and experiences. They will automatically engage both hemispheres, and the more we can do to support such efforts, the better their learning will be.[78] We need to help them take the time and effort to utilize the executive center of their brains which will better engage their higher-order thinking capabilities.

The human brain is a social brain and learns best when working with others. It needs time to think, to reflect, and to integrate what it is learning or experiencing. It needs mental breaks. Multiple avenues of teaching and learning need to be incorporated as some students are primarily visual learners (40–65 percent) and others are auditory (25–30 percent) or kinesthetic (5–15 percent). The brain seeks to make connections to previous memories and experiences. It wants relevancy and novelty, and the brain is always looking for patterns and relationships in order to understand the big picture. As such, the brain can adapt.

In other words, we need to give students opportunities to stretch those advanced areas of their brains, to think about their own thinking strategies—metacognition—and we need—as discipline specialists—to model these behaviors for them. In turn, this understanding of how the brain works will impact our curriculum, our pedagogy, our classroom environment, and how we assess our students, as well as the effectiveness of our own teaching.

The Classroom and Its Environment

The classroom needs to provide an environment that supports what we know best about how the brain learns. If a student should feel threatened by an intimidating teaching style or being embarrassed in front of their classmates, they will be stuck in a primitive low-level cognitive mode. We expect higher order thinking, so we need to create an atmosphere that supports it.

This means we need to focus on the learner and their learning. We need to move from teacher-oriented classrooms and instruction to one that supports learning. K–12 teachers have for quite some time helped to create a learner-centered classroom where students take on more ownership of their own learning. Some teachers have even now moved beyond the phrase "*learner*-centered" to the notion of "*learning*-centered" classrooms.

In either case, professors will want to ensure their classrooms aren't intimidating places that create high levels of stress. Students need to be able to feel comfortable enough to struggle with ideas and to explore their own thinking and the topics at hand without the worry of reprisal from the professor or fellow classmates. Students need to be free to make mistakes and learn from them. While some stress may be beneficial—in the form of challenge—we must not create an atmosphere whereby students just want to escape. We need to think in terms of high challenge, but low stress. Eric Jensen stipulates that up to 90 percent of the input our brains receive enters at the unconscious level.[79] The classroom environment is critical.

We know that the human brain is a social brain. People often learn best by their interactions with others, or social learning. The key takeaway here, however, is the need for students to have opportunities to work with one another at some point during the lesson. Students learn different approaches from their peers, and they learn better by sharing their own approaches, as well. Likewise, the professor needs to be responsive to the needs of all learners.

Zaretta Hammond[80] provides an informative framework for teaching students with cultural responsiveness to engage the brain. Her research emphasizes that the brain must feel safe and culturally considered because, to a certain degree, our brains are uploaded with cultural "software" due to the cultural norms that we have been exposed to throughout our lives.

These cultural norms that we were exposed to since birth essentially contribute to our realities and dispositions toward the world. Therefore, the "hardware" of our brains will respond to environmental stimuli because of how that stimuli aligns with our cultural understandings of the world. Thus, the cultural responsiveness or lack thereof in a classroom environment can influence the fight, flight, and freeze response.

John Bransford and his colleagues have put together a short list of practices they recommend be instituted for today's classrooms. It provides an erudite summation of the implications covered over the previous pages. This list is paraphrased with interpretation as follows:

1. Schools and classrooms must be learner-centered with the focus on each student and their learning. This requires an approach of differentiation in teaching practices. Faculty need to present students with "just manageable difficulties." This means tasks need to be challenging enough to maintain engagement but not so difficult as to lead to discouragement.
2. Attention must be given to what is taught (information, subject matter), why it is taught (understanding), and what competence or mastery looks like. Learning with understanding is often harder to accomplish than simply memorizing, and it takes more time. We must disabuse ourselves of a curriculum that is a mile wide and an inch deep. Focus must be given to essential concepts with in-depth study and understanding. Likewise, our tests often reinforce memorizing rather than understanding. So, we will need to look to better align our testing approaches with higher-level thinking.
3. Formative assessment needs to play an ever-increasing role in our classrooms. Real-time formative assessments are those quick and informal checks designed to determine student understanding as lessons progress. Such assessments help both the professor and the student determine if they're on the right track or whether more instruction is needed.
4. Quizzes for the sake of grading are not as relevant. "Gotcha quizzes" are less appropriate and unnecessary where students have ownership in their own learning. In sum, formative assessments provide students with opportunities to revise and improve their thinking, helps students see their own progress, and help teachers identify problems that need to be remedied.
5. Learning is influenced in fundamental ways by the context in with it takes place. An authentic real-life community-centered approach requires development of norms for the classroom and school, as well as connections to the outside world that support core learning values, build on contributions of individual members, and confer a sense of ownership.[81]

All these implications are natural extensions from what we know about how students' brains learn. These require students to take more ownership and responsibility for their own learning. The classroom needs to be a place conducive to challenge without negative stress and a place for social interaction. The student experience needs to show relevance, to be authentic, and to be contextually based. The best professors are already using many of these practices, and such teaching practices can be very rewarding. Part III will show how.

The Curriculum

The curriculum is the domain of the faculty—the experts in the content area. What we have learned about the brain will have direct impact, however, on how these experts structure what they teach, how they teach it, the work they assign, and how they assess the effectiveness of their instruction. In so doing, professors need to help their students connect to previous learning and memories, to scaffold these experiences, and to make learning opportunities authentic, contextual, and experiential, wherever possible.

Well-designed learning activities do more than simply present information. They help students engage with the content and guide students to connect previous memories and experiences in order to help construct, scaffold, and integrate the new. We know that memory improves through practice, and therefore professors need to provide opportunities for students to practice and struggle with new concepts. The brain is capable of memorizing a great deal of information, but learning through trial and error and integration is ultimately more efficient. When developing lesson plans or units of instruction, professors should keep in mind the hierarchical levels of learning according to Bloom's Taxonomy. This will help focus the curriculum and instruction on higher-level skills and intellectual engagement.

Student learning becomes more effective as they become aware and critical of their own thinking and their previous assumptions.[82] It is imperative that instructors help students incorporate metacognitive practices as part of their learning routines. As such, professors need to model their own thinking with their students and to lead them to become self-motivated—to take ownership of their own learning. In modeling, instructors show their own thinking out loud, how they grapple with subjects, and how they arrive at their well-considered decisions. Such practices mirror those attributes of critical thinking.

Certainly, one primary goal for teachers is to help students to move short-term and working memory into long-term memory. One method is for students to put into their own words, via writing, speaking, or presenting, what they have learned. In addition, while we know repetition of specific facts is a relatively ineffective way to learn, students do learn new information more easily and remember it longer when they connect it with things they already know, as well as to things that are context- and real-life based. Further, learning is enhanced by emphasizing the big picture, and then allowing students to discover the details for themselves.

Whether or not our students can attain expertise in the subject matter, we are reminded of the work by Bransford and his colleagues about characteristics of outstanding students. They have learned to notice features and meaningful patterns of information that are not recognized by novices. They have acquired a great deal of content knowledge that is organized in ways that reflect a deep understanding of their subject matter. Their knowledge cannot be reduced to sets of isolated facts or propositions but instead reflects contexts of applicability—that is, their knowledge is "conditionalized" on a set of circumstances. Finally, they are able to flexibly retrieve important aspects of their knowledge with little attentional effort.[83]

The most important takeaways are that professors need to help students understand the applicability of contextualized learning by seeing the whole picture, first. Further, they must dive deep into the given topic in order to understand it thoroughly and to develop a conceptualization of patterns and relationships—to make sense of the content. Students need to realize the connections from the parts to the whole, and to see the relevance, in other words.

As students take ownership for their learning, professors need to keep in mind motivational principals elucidated in Maslow's Needs Hierarchy. The focus needs to be on learning and not teaching. To paraphrase Paulo Freire, "Don't take away the dignity of their struggle."[84] The students need time to process, to reflect—to think about what they are learning. Physical space and time must be given so they can make these requisite intellectual connections and leaps.

Our best students are self-disciplined, prefer complexity and realistic activity, but enjoy high challenge, and take ownership and responsibility for their own learning. Such classroom environments and curriculum drive pedagogy of the best professors.

Pedagogy

Pedagogy is *how* we teach our content to the students. While professors are experts in their fields, they too often have been given little time in understanding and preparing how to teach their content. In fact, most professors teach the way they were taught—their mimetic isomorphism. It's the only approach they have ever seen, so it's the only way they know how to approach their instruction. Once in the profession of teaching, most of their time is spent in continued content engagement or scholarship. Still, what we have learned about brain research can change *how* we teach.

Contemporary learning theories and subsequent pedagogical strategies will be further developed in Part II. However, some key concepts are worth exploring presently. Professors William McKeachie and Marilla Svinicki explain the proper perspective:

> What is important is learning, not teaching. Teaching effectiveness depends not just on what the teacher does, but rather on what the student does. Teaching involves listening as much as talking. It's important that both teacher and students are actively thinking, but most important is what goes on in the students' minds. Those minds are not blank slates. They hold expectations, experiences, and conceptions that will shape their interpretation of the knowledge you present. Your task is to help them develop mental representations of your subject matter that will provide a basis for further learning, thinking, and use.[85]

Robert Leamnson expresses, "If learning is indeed a matter of brain development—synapses stabilized through use—it becomes equally clear that it cannot be effected by anyone but the learner."[86] Thus, while learning causes changes in the brains—strengthens neural connections and makes memories and subsequent recall easier and more interconnected, it is the student who must take control, ownership, and ultimate responsibility for their own learning. This is certainly true for college students. In *What the Best College Professors Do*, Ken Bain concludes:

> The best college and university teachers create what we might call a natural critical learning environment in which they embed the skills and information they wish to teach in assignments . . . authentic tasks that will arouse curiosity, challenging students to rethink their assumptions and examine their mental models of reality. They create a safe environment in which students can try, come up short, receive feedback, and try again. Students understand and remember what they have learned because they master and use the reasoning abilities necessary to integrate it with larger concepts.[87]

When we teach, we need to take advantage of the unconscious mind and the inclination of emotion to engage learners and to connect with previous learning experiences and memories. We need to train students to slow down, to reflect, and to engage the executive center of their brains—to be mindful in how they approach their learning.

Students' brains actively seek to engage the content in order to construct and scaffold their learning. Useful, practical, and functional knowledge is based on activity. People build new knowledge by using their brain actively to solve real-world problems or real-life situations. Since human brains are social brains, we need to take advantage of the social environment of our classrooms and create opportunities for students to work with one another.

The best instructors use differentiation in teaching strategies to deal with the various learning styles of their students. The students themselves can help do this. Students can explicitly show their peers how they approach and solve problems. In turn, students will learn a variety of ways to resolve issues and which approaches are optimal.

In addition, when a student verbalizes or puts in writing their understanding of a concept or how they solve a problem, they are forced to be clear and precise—to themselves. The feedback they receive from their classmates, indeed their own reflecting, will likely force better understanding. In other words, students not only learn from each other, but they learn from themselves through the process of metacognition and explanation whether in speaking, in writing, or in action.

We need to avoid long lectures. Only 5 to 10 percent of information imparted during a lecture is retained after just one day. Discussion is a more effective way of ensuring retention. Teachers need to grab their students' attention, or at least show its relevance, within the first twenty seconds of introducing a new subject and should captivate their students with a topic that is meaningful, according to Eric Jensen and Liesl McConchie. These authors differentiate between episodic and semantic learning:

> Explicit inputs are initiated by life experiences—or what we, as educators might call direct instruction. Episodic learning is usually rich in sensory information, and therefore our discussion of sensory inputs involves [various] processes, systems, and structures . . . [and] often includes the brain's emotional headquarters. . . . Semantic learning, on the other hand, is often less sense-enriched unless a teacher is highly skilled in the art of differentiated instruction. A traditional lecture will only involve the language systems of and structures of the brain.., with the occasional inclusion of visual systems and structures . . . when visual presentations are used.[88]

Cognition and memories are strengthened, as a matter of fact, by rich experiences and by activating multiple regions of the brain using the different senses. The more senses involved and the more experiences we have, the greater the ability to remember and to think at higher levels. Most learners, 40–65 percent, would be considered visual learners, as noted earlier. Auditory learners comprise another 25–30 percent, and 5–15 percent are primarily kinesthetic learners. The more ways we can help students access our content, the more likely they will learn.

Students need to connect working memory with long-term memory by linking the present situation to past experiences. Moreover, evidence suggests the value of teaching content in small chunk sizes. Research says two to four chunks are realistic in terms of the capacity for working memory. More than that, students are unable to make the transition from the immediate memory to the long-term.

The learning task must be authentic and geared toward real-life and problem-solving activities for the students. Teaching content in isolation from reality makes understanding all the more difficult. Moreover, Piaget emphasized that the learner's brain can more readily accommodate new knowledge when it is able to reach into its stores of memories, better known as schemas, and connect the new knowledge to its preexisting knowledge. When this accommodation does not happen, disequilibrium ensues.

In their work published by the National Academy Press, John Bransford and his colleagues perhaps sum this section up best with "Implications for Teaching":

1. "Teachers must draw out and work with the preexisting understandings that their students bring with them. The teacher must actively inquire into students' thinking creating classroom tasks and conditions under which student thinking can be revealed. The roles for assessment must be expanded beyond the traditional concept of testing. . . . Frequent formative assessment helps make students' thinking visible to themselves and their teachers." Such assessments will focus more on high-order thinking and activities.
2. Teachers must focus on depth rather than breadth in their instruction. This will reach higher level cognitive processes and learning. Assessment will subsequently take on a new focus with fewer multiple choice and other factual exams and more reality-based performance examinations. Such examinations are difficult to prepare and have a more subjective rather than objective basis.

3. Teachers must help students learn metacognitive skills so they can independently master their own reflective practices.[89] They need to think about their own thinking, to reflect and challenge their own assumptions, and to critically examine how they arrive at their conclusions.

Finally, the effectiveness of our teaching and the success of our students' learning needs to be measured and analyzed, or assessed, if you will. A combined strategy of formative and summative assessment of both our teaching and of the students' learning must be examined in toto.

Assessment

Summative assessment, as the name implies, is typically an evaluation given in summation or as a summary of learning at the end of a unit of study. These are often associated with formal grades and at times may be considered high stakes—to determine a student's final grade, their ability to pass a course, or as a comprehensive exam, for example.

Formative assessments are more ongoing throughout a given period of time, say a unit of study, and can be either formal or informal. Grades may or may not be associated with formative assessments. They are designed to quickly determine students' grasp of material, quality of instruction, and whether additional instruction is necessary. Such assessments help both the instructor and the student check their progress.

In a very real sense, the ways in which teachers assess students' learning influence what and how students actually learn. In other words, what and how students learn depend, in part, on how they expect their learning to be assessed. What gets assessed gets taught and learned. As such, professors need to grapple with the purpose of grading. Is it to determine whether a student should successfully pass the course, or is its purpose to make teaching adjustments and provide feedback to the students, for example?

The best exams should, like assignments, be learning experiences as well as evaluative mechanisms. Professors lose valuable opportunities to advance student learning when they use a grade as merely a culminating marker. After an exam is given, there is a prime opportunity for the instructor to review the correct answers with the class. Often students will guess at answers and might get them correct without ever really knowing. Reviewing the answers is an opportunity to correct understanding and misunderstanding.

Finally, how students receive assessment feedback can be equally important. Again, they may have a fight or flight response to feedback if it is handled in a stressful manner. If this is the case, the professor loses an opportunity for a learning experience. If students just want to get away from the feedback, they won't be in an emotional position to receive it—to learn from it. So, we need to be careful how they receive our communication; we don't want to make the students defensive. In other words, the goal is to focus on feedback as a learning experience, not simply a pro forma reporting mechanism.

SUMMARY

In sum, the lessons we have learned about how the brain works can have significant implications for our curriculum, the way we teach, our classroom environments, and how we assess both the students' learning and the subsequent effectiveness of our instruction.

As we know, most students have a left-brain or right-brain propensity for learning, for thinking, and for processing information. As such, students prefer certain personal approaches to learning. So, too, professors have preferred ways to teach. The best instructors find ways to reach all their learners—to differentiate their instruction.

We have learned that left-brain-dominate students are most comfortable learning through reading, writing, and speaking. They prefer linear and sequential thinking moving from parts to the whole. They need to analyze all the facts before understanding how concepts come together. They prefer structured and orderly classrooms. Left brain professors use lecture notes and agendas. They are orderly, well-managed, on time, and their lessons are well-structured and predictable. Conversely, right brain learners wish their professors used illustrations and discussions.

Right-brain students are comfortable with emotions, feelings, and intuition. They learn from novel thinking. It is here where options are explored, images are visualized, and imagination is nurtured. They prefer to see things moving from the whole to the parts. They are global, big picture learners. They prefer melody, pattern recognition, intuition, and spontaneity, and are tolerant of ambiguity and unpredictable situations. These professors use visuals, diagrams, and hands-on lessons, along with discussions and problem-based learning. In these classrooms, left-brain learners want more structure, organization, and predictability.[90]

Geoffrey and Renate Caine have condensed all these lessons into seven principles for application of the brain-compatible adult classroom. In part, these are:[91]

1. *Learning is collaborative and influenced by interactions with others*: The human brain is a social brain. Professors need to allow learners to select their own flexible seating with and encourage differential groupings for students to engage with one another—to learn from one another. Interacting out loud forces students to clarify, justify, and extend their thinking.
2. *The adult brain creates meaning by linking past to present into familiar patterns*: Adult learners want to engage by actively challenging concepts in order to make sense of the content. This process helps them to connect to existing neural networks. The new knowledge then becomes integrated into the learner's existing knowledge and creates opportunity for scaffolding. The brain processes information both sequentially and holistically through communication between the hemispheres as the entire brain interacts as a dynamic whole.
3. *Emotions and stress can adversely impact learning*: The brain is heavily influenced by emotional stimuli. The brain makes greater synaptic connections between neurons when it is appropriately challenged with novel experiences. However, under stressful or threatening conditions, the student's brain may shift down to the primitive region where survival is the main focus. As a result, learners are less likely to tap into their higher-order thinking and creativity when negative emotions surface. Educators can promote higher-level learning by encouraging self-efficacy and creating an environment of relaxed alertness, which involves low threat and high challenge.
4. *Adults learn through both conscious, focused attention and unconscious, peripheral processing*: Most learning takes place at the subconscious level. Professors need to make efforts to have students reflect upon what they have learned and to creatively elaborate on their reflections, ideas, and experiences to make the learning more meaningful. In other words, they need to help make the implicit explicit. At the same time, the brain also needs frequent breaks from direct, focused attention to process information in a more effective manner. A nonstop flow of information, such as in the traditional lecture, may actually be counterproductive to the natural way the brain learns. Regular breaks every twenty to

thirty minutes are beneficial. Opportunities to talk informally with others about what they learned is an excellent strategy.

5. *Adult learners process information through multiple memory pathways*: The best instructors encourage learners to integrate what they are learning into their own personal life experiences and then encourage learners to relate new concepts to past experiences and prerequisite knowledge. This scaffolding approach helps students to construct a comprehensive and integrated approach to learning. Eliciting emotions is a prime way to tie into previous experiences. Fortunately, adult learners enjoy a plethora of real-life prior experiences to bring to the college classroom environment. Professors need to take advantage of this.
6. *The adult brain is uniquely organized and never stops learning*: Neural plasticity is an advantage of the adult learner. Professors should use a variety of teaching modalities (auditory, visual, and kinesthetic) to help their adult students bring in previous learning and life experiences and make connections across brain networks. Giving students multiple opportunities to present their understanding of new concepts, to discuss with other students, and to create physical representations are all simple ways to support these different modes.
7. *A healthy lifestyle contributes to optimal learning*: Some of these principles are more or less out of the instructor's control. However, professors can encourage the students to get plenty of sleep[92]—a very difficult challenge for the working professional; to get adequate physical exercise—another difficult challenge for the working adult; and, to eat healthy. Perhaps the best advice is for students to be properly hydrated. Professors can support this effort by permitting students to have water in the classroom or to take routine refreshment breaks. Once students begin to show signs of distraction, it is a good time for a physical break. This allows not only a chance to stretch and get rehydrated, but it is also an opportunity to think about what has just been learned—as noted in principle four.

Together, all that we have learned about the brain should have tremendous impact on how we teach our students. At the same time, educators and cognitive scientists have spent years pondering the questions about how students learn best and, in turn, how teachers should reach their students. Learning theory and cognition, the work of these considered professionals, is the focus of Part II. Most interestingly, there are models, and parts of models, that are best supported by what we have learned from brain research, and together they can help students construct their own learning.

NOTES

1. Olaf Sporns, *Networks of the Brain* (Cambridge, MA: MIT Press, 2011). In terms of learning and how the brain functions, "There is no learned skill that uses only one part of the brain, and there is no one part of the brain with a singular function. Instead, the brain systems that support learning and academic skills are the same brain systems that are integral to personhood—that is, to social, cognitive, emotional, and cultural functioning and even to health and physiological survival." Mary Helen Immordino-Yang and Rebecca Gotlieb, "Embodied Brains, Social Minds, Cultural Meaning: Integrating Neuroscientific and Educational Research on Social-Affective Development," *American Educational Research Journal: Centennial Issue* 54, no. 1 (2017): 344S–367S. http://journals.sagepub.com/doi/abs/10.3102/0002831216669780. Cited in: Institute of Medicine, *From Neurons to Neighborhoods: The Science of Early Childhood Development* (Washington, DC: National Academy Press, 2000).

2. Richard Restak, *The New Brain: How the Modern Age is Rewiring Your Brain* (Emmaus, PA: Rodale Press, 2003), 125. Restack goes on to note: "Rather than the gene itself, the ultimate determiner of genetic fate is the network of connections and reactions within the cell" (125). It is not a matter of good or bad genes but, rather, the networks interacting with one another throughout the brain.

3. Jane Healy, *Your Child's Growing Mind: Brain Development and Learning from Birth to Adolescence* (New York: Broadway Books, 2007), 8.

4. Institute of Medicine, *From Neurons to Neighborhoods: The Science of Early Childhood Development* (Washington, DC: National Academy Press, 2000); The National Academies of Sciences, Engineering, and Medicine *How People Learn II: Learners, Contexts, and Cultures* (Washington, DC: National Academies Press, 2018), 56, https://doi.org/10.17226/24783, cited research of the National Research Council and Institute of Medicine, *Transforming the Workforce for Children Birth Through Age 8: A Unifying Foundation* (Washington, DC: National Academies Press, 2015); and Gerry Leisman, Raed Mualem, and Safa Khayat Mughrabi, "The Neurological Development of the Child with the Educational Enrichment in Mind" *Psicología Educativa* 21, no. 2 (2015): 79–96, https://doi.org/10.1016/j.pse.2015.08.006.

[Among the key findings of early brain development and its affects on lifelong learning]:
- Experience and genetics both contribute to observed variability in human development.
- The human brain develops from conception through the early twenties and beyond in an orderly progression. Vital and autonomic functions develop first, then cognitive, motor, sensory, and perceptual processes, with complex integrative processes and value-driven and long-term decision making developing last.
- Early adversity can have important short- and long-term effects on the brain's development and other essential functions.

5. Rhosel Lenroot and Jay Giedd, "Brain Development in Children and Adolescents: Insights from Anatomical Magnetic Resonance Imaging," *Neuroscience Biobehavioral Review* 30, no. 6 (2006): 718–29.

6. Robert Sylwester, *A Celebration of Neurons: An Educator's Guide to the Human Brain* (Alexandria, VA: Association of Supervision and Curriculum Development, 1995), 127–28.

7. Eric Jensen and Liesl McConchie, *Brain-Based Learning: Teaching the Way Students Really Learn* (Thousand Oaks, CA: Corwin, 2020), 16. Jensen and McConchie elaborated on the systems involved in healthy brain functioning by including: digestive, respiratory, nervous, circulatory, and sympathetic and parasympathetic (15).

8. Sylwester, *A Celebration of Neurons*, 27.

9. Sylwester, *A Celebration of Neurons*, 75.

10. John Medaglia, Mary-Ellen Lynall, and Danielle Bassett, "Cognitive Network Neuroscience," *Journal of Cognitive Neuroscience* 27, no. 8 (2015): 1471–91.

11. Healy, *Your Child's Growing Mind*, 20.

12. Healy, *Your Child's Growing Mind*, 230. For example, the limbic system, the hippocampus, the amygdala, and the cerebral cortex all play critical roles in memory depending on the type of stimulus.

13. Sylwester, *A Celebration of Neurons*, 89.

14. Michio Kaku, *The Future of the Mind: The Scientific Quest to Understand, Enhance, and Empower the Mind* (New York: Doubleday, 2014), 123–24.

15. National Academies, *How People Learn II*, 75.

16. Mihalyi Csikszentmihalyi, *Flow: The Psychology of Optimal Experience* (New York: Harper Collins, 1990), 26.

17. Daniel Levitin, *This Is Your Brain on Music: The Science of a Human Obsession* (New York: Plume of Penguin Group, 2006), 57. Levitin adds: "Musical activity involves nearly every region of the brain that we know about, and nearly every neural subsystem" (85–86).

18. Laurie Materna, *Jump Start the Adult Learner: How to Engage and Motivate Adults Using Brain-Compatible Strategies* (Thousand Oaks, CA: Corwin Press, 2007), 3–9. A brief and very generalized paraphrased description of the brain systems follows below. Much greater detail is provided later in the part along with implications for educators.

The lower brain is made up of the brain stem and the cerebellum. This is the brain's first region to mature and is primarily responsible for survival, for much of our sensory data, for basic bodily regulation, for motor movement, and to communicate with the middle brain, among other responsibilities. Should a person perceive threats to their survival, impulses to the lower brain will not continue to move to the more advanced areas of the brain—indeed, classroom learning will likely not occur.

The middle brain is made up of the limbic system: amygdala, hippocampus, and the thalamus. It is known as the portion of the brain regulating hormones and our emotions. It communicates with the thinking part of the brain as well as the motor part. Our senses, with the exception of smell, are regulated here, and many of our memories are stored here. Much of our short-term memories, working knowledge, and attention are stored and activated in the middle brain. This region of the brain works with the prefrontal cortex to determine the response to stimuli found by our senses and to our emotions.

The upper brain is made up of the cerebrum and is covered by the neocortex. This is the last portion of the brain to develop and is where most of our thinking is done. It is divided into two hemispheres and four lobes: frontal, occipital, parietal, and temporal. The two hemispheres are connected by a thick nerve fiber—the corpus callosum which serves as the communication link between the hemispheres and the lobes. While each hemisphere and each lobe have primary functions, each is intimately integrated with one another. No thinking is done without the interactions of the others.

19. Colin Rose, *Accelerated Learning Action Guide* (Aylesbury Buckinghamshire, UK: Accelerated Learning Systems, 1995). This document was cited in Materna, *Jump Start the Adult Learner*, 29.
20. Healy, *Your Child's Growing Mind*, 372.
21. Kaku, *The Future of the Mind*, 220.
22. Neurotransmitters are natural chemicals which include: dopamine, serotonin, norepinephrine.
23. Materna, *Jump Start the Adult Learner*, 24. Materna added a hopeful insight: "the brain not only creates new cells, throughout a lifetime but . . . the new cells live longer and grow stronger when the brain is actively engaged in new learning. This research is particularly exciting in terms of adult learning and supports the need for promoting learning activities that naturally engage adults' motivation, interests, and attention by drawing upon personal experiences" (24).
24. National Academies of Sciences, Engineering, and Medicine, *How People Learn II: Learners, Contexts, and Cultures* (Washington, DC: National Academies Press, 2018), 4, https://doi.org/10.17226/24783.
25. Sylwester, *A Celebration of Neurons*, 89.
26. Restak, *The New Brain*, 32.
27. Evan Thompson, *Waking, Dreaming, Being: Self and Consciousness in Neuroscience, Meditation, and Philosophy* (New York: Columbia University Press, 2017), 342 and 343.
28. Michael Talbot *The Holographic Universe* (New York: Harper Collins, 1991), 20.
29. Sylwester, *A Celebration of Neurons*, 120.
30. Jeanne Ellis Ormrod and Brett Jones, *Essentials of Educational Psychology* (New York: Pearson, 2019), 210. The authors elaborate: "In the cortex—and especially the prefrontal cortex—synaptic pruning continues into the middle childhood and adolescent years, a second wave of synaptogenesis occurs at puberty, and myelination continues into early adulthood. And several parts of the brain, especially those that are heavily involved in thinking and learning, continue to increase in size and interconnections until late adolescence or early adulthood" (211).
31. National Academies, *How People Learn II*, 70.
32. Levitin, *This Is Your Brain on Music*, 185.
33. Sylwester, *A Celebration of Neurons*, 95.
34. Andrew Holecek, *Dream Yoga: Illuminating Your Life through Lucid Dreaming and the Tibetan Yogas of Sleep* (Boulder, CO: Sounds True, 2016).
35. Materna, *Jump Start the Adult Learner*. For greater detail to the discussion of the lower, middle, and upper portions of the brain and implications for educational practices, the reader is invited to read Part I of Materna's book.
36. Materna, *Jump Start the Adult Learner*, 34.

37. Sylwester, *A Celebration of Neurons*, 113. In other words, emotions take precedence unless we purposefully take the time to reflect and be judicial.

38. Fred Alan Wolf, *The Dreaming Universe: A Mind-Expanding Journey into the Realm Where Psyche and Physics Meet* (New York: Touchstone of Simon & Schuster, 1994), 96.

39. Materna, *Jump Start the Adult Learner*, 8. Materna adds that the hippocampus works with factual, or semantic memories, while the amygdala is responsible for memories associated with our emotions; Healy (*Your Child's Growing Mind*) further explains: "The hippocampus mediates factual memory and the amygdala attaches emotional significance to experience so that we can quickly classify a stimulus as potentially dangerous." Thus, "the limbic system, can either facilitate learning or block the thinking systems" (243).

40. Institute of Medicine, *From Neurons to Neighborhoods: The Science of Early Childhood Development* (Washington, DC: National Academy Press, 2000).

41. Ellis Ormrod and Jones, *Essentials of Educational Psychology*, 23.

42. Jensen and McConchie, *Brain-Based Learning*, 102.

43. Ellis Ormrod and Jones, *Essentials of Educational Psychology*, 22. According to the authors, the prefrontal cortex doesn't reach maturity until humans reach their early twenties (210).

44. Bloom's Taxonomy of Learning is discussed in detail in Part III.

45. Sylwester, *A Celebration of Neurons*, 54.

46. Andrew Holecek. *Dream Yoga: Illuminating Your Life through Lucid Dreaming and the Tibetan Yogas of Sleep* (Boulder, CO: Sounds True. 2016), 272.

47. For a detailed yet erudite explanation of how the system of neurons interconnect as individual pieces to form into a cogent understanding of a full picture or understanding, the reader is encouraged to read Sylwester, *A Celebration of Neurons*, Part II.

48. Materna, *Jump Start the Adult Learner*, 22.

49. Douglas Hacker, "Failures to Detect Textual Problems during Reading," in *Processing Inaccurate Information: Theoretical and Implied Perspectives from Cognitive Science and the Educational Sciences*, edited by David Rapp and Jason Braasch (Cambridge, MA: The MIT Press, 2014), 88.

50. Sylwester, *A Celebration of Neurons*, 49.

51. Ellis Ormrod and Jones, *Essentials of Educational Psychology*, 22.

52. Materna, *Jump Start the Adult Learner*, 14.

53. Kaku, *The Future of the Mind*, 37. With regard to left-brain dominance, Kaku expresses an interesting take on brain injuries and on autistic behavior: "Normally, the left brain restricts this talent [the creative side of the right brain] and holds it in check. But if the left brain is injured in a certain way, it may unleash the artistic abilities latent in the right brain, causing an explosion of artistic talent" (145). Others have speculated that certain drugs may inhibit the dominant authority of the left-brain providing opportunity for artistic expression. Others have even suggested that the left side of the brain becomes less dominant when we sleep which allows more right brain activity, hence stranger dreams.

54. Holecek, *Dream Yoga*, 14. Holecek goes on to note: "Researchers at Georgetown University discovered that during naps, the right hemisphere of the brain, which is associated with creativity, is very active, while the left hemisphere, which is more analytical, is relatively quiet. The left hemisphere, which tends to dominate the right, specializes in numbers and language processing. It's almost as if when the chattering and reasoning left hemisphere shuts up, the creative right hemisphere opens up" (14).

55. Leonard Shlain, *The Alphabet Versus the Goddess: The Conflict Between Word and Image* (New York: Penguin Group, 1998), 17 and 23.

56. Restak, *The New Brain*, 72, for example expressed, "If you're driving in unfamiliar surroundings while glancing down at a map, it's primarily your right hemisphere that processes the lines and figures on the map. But if, instead, someone in the passenger seat is telling you directions, your left hemisphere is the primary processor of the verbal description of your route" (72).

57. Healy, *Your Child's Growing Mind*, 336.

58. Materna, *Jump Start the Adult Learner*, 17.

59. Yongman Chang, "Reorganization and Plastic Changes of the Human Brain Associated with Skill Learning and Expertise," *Frontiers in Human Neuroscience* 8, no. 35 (2014), https://doi.org/10.3389

/fnhum.2014.00035; Sara Bengtsson, Zoltan Nagy, Stefan Skare, Lea Forsman, Hans Forssberg, and Fredrik Ullen, "Extensive Piano Practicing Has Regionally Specific Effects on White Matter Development," *Nature Neuroscience* 8, no. 9 (2005): 1148–50.

60. John Bransford, Ann Brown, and Rodney Cocking, eds., *How People Learn: Brain, Mind, Experience, and School* (Washington, DC: National Academy Press, 2000), 31. Often, experts are considered expert in their field because of their vast experience in the content field, besides their high degree of training. In addition, "Experts look for patterns and chunk information. . . . They organize key concepts around big ideas and concepts and relationships—part of chunking, look at alternative solutions" (36).

61. Healy, *Your Child's Growing Mind*, 351–52.

62. Sylwester, *A Celebration of Neurons*, 112.

63. Levitin, *This Is Your Brain on Music*, 125. Levitin added: "The front portion of the corpus callosum . . . is significantly larger in musicians than nonmusicians. . . . This reinforces the notion that musical operations become bilateral with increased training, as musicians coordinate and recruit neural structures in both the left and right hemispheres" (226).

64. Restak, *The New Brain*, 4.

65. Restak, *The New Brain*, 24–26.

66. Restak, *The New Brain*, 14. The reader is invited to a fascinating read of Part II—"Genius and Superior Performance: Are We All Capable?" of Restak's book as it is devoted to an exhaustive study of genius musicians, chess masters, athletes, and others.

67. Restak, *The New Brain*, 15. Restak believes, among other researchers, that expertise is less a matter of innate qualities, and more a matter of hard work, determination, focus, and the ability to self-direction and self-control. They are flexible in their thinking and problem-solving and are constantly seeking to improve. They are their own best or toughest judges. Like Healy, Materna, and others, Restak cites those with superior performance exhibiting traits of "flow" as coined by Mihalyi Cziskzentmihalyi.

68. Restak, *The New Brain*, 21. Restak went on to explain similar attributes in musicians: "Musically sophisticated individuals are more likely to perceive music in an analytical manner and thus rely more heavily on their dominant (usually left) hemisphere" (98).

69. Gail Davies, Max Lam, Sarah Harris, Joey Trampush, Michelle Luciano, and W. David Hill, "Study of 300,486 Individuals Identifies 148 Independent Genetic Loci Influencing General Cognitive Function," *Nat Communications* 9, no. 1 (2018): 1 16.

70. David Bueno, "Genetics and Learning: How the Genes Influence Educational Attainment," *Frontiers in Psychology* 10 (2019): 1–10.

71. Kaili Rimfeld, Z. Ayorech, P. Dale, Y. Kovas, and R. Plomin, "Genetics Affects Choice of Academic Subjects as well as Achievement," *Scientific Reports* 6 (2016): 1–9.

72. Bueno, "Genetics and Learning," 7.

73. Bueno, "Genetics and Learning."

74. Sylwester, *A Celebration of Neurons*, 129–30.

75. Jensen and McConchie, *Brain-Based Learning*, 86

76. Jensen and McConchie, *Brain-Based Learning*, 102. They concluded, "Your students' brains will naturally prioritize emotional processes over academic content. Students who are preoccupied with something emotional, not related to the learning, will struggle" (103); Wolf drove home the critical necessity of emotions to learning: "Feelings create emotions, and emotions are vital to having any memory at all. In other words, we do not remember anything that we have no feelings about." Fred Alan Wolf, *The Dreaming Universe: A Mind-Expanding Journey into the Realm Where Psyche and Physics Meet* (New York: Touchstone, 1994): 45.

77. Healy, *Your Child's Growing Mind*.

78. Materna, *Jump Start the Adult Learner*. "All in all, whole-brain learning uses the creative-intuitive mind as well as the critical-logical mind to accomplish a variety of learning goals" (19).

79. Jensen and McConchie, *Brain-Based Learning*, 147–48. To which they added: "Three factors that operate at non-conscious level that are needed for optimal brain performance and learning: (1) Safety, (2) Belonging, (3) Hope and support. Students who have a sense of belonging to a school or classroom

community are more likely to engage in positive academic behaviors that produce higher levels of engagement and performance. And Do I fit in? Do people care about me? Am I valued?" (152).

80. Zaretta Hammond, *Culturally Responsive Teaching and the Brain: Promoting Authentic Engagement and Rigor Among Culturally and Linguistically Diverse Students* (New York: Corwin Press, 2015).

81. Bransford et al., *How People Learn*, 23–25.

82. Levitin, *This Is Your Brain on Music*: "The brain makes errors, so students need to confront their previous understandings and to correct where needed. According to Levitin: "The brain constructs a representation of reality, based on . . . component features. . . . In the process, the brain makes a number of inferences, due to incomplete or ambiguous information; sometimes these inferences turn out to be wrong" (105). Initially, the professor can help students reflect upon previous understanding and assumptions. Eventually, students can learn metacognitive practices in order to deconstruct faulty learning so they can then construct new learning upon a sound foundation.

83. Bransford et al., *How People Learn*, 31.

84. Paulo Freire, *Pedagogy of the Oppressed* (New York: Continuum International Publishing, 1970).

85. Wilbert McKeachie and Marilla Svinicki, *Teaching Tips: Strategies, Research, and Theory for College and University Teachers* (Boston: Houghton-Mifflin, 2006), 6.

86. Robert Leamnson, *Thinking about Teaching and Learning: Developing Habits of Learning with First Year College and University Students* (Sterling, VA: Sylus Publishing, 1999), 18.

87. Ken Bain, *What the Best College Teachers Do* (Cambridge, MA: Harvard University Press, 2004), 47.

88. Jensen and McConchie, *Brain-Based Learning*, 24–25.

89. Bransford et al., *How People Learn*, 19–21. Paraphrased by the authors of this book.

90. Materna, *Jump Start the Adult Learner*, 15–16. These descriptions of left- and right-brain students and teachers are paraphrased from the work of Materna.

91. Renate Nummela and Geoffrey Caine, "Understanding a Brain-Based Approach to Learning and Teaching" (Alexandria, VA: *Educational Leadership*. Association for Supervision and Curriculum Development, 1990), 66–70. The text in italics comes from the Caines, while the text that follows it is combined paraphrasing and commentary of the authors of this book.

92. "Activation of the hippocampus (which plays a key role in memory integration) during sleep seems to allow connections between memory traces to be formed across the cortex" (National Academies, *How People Learn II*, 87).

Part II

Learning Theory

Now that we have discussed how the brain learns—its numerous processes of thinking and reacting to its environment, we can address the three foundational learning theories from which essentially all teaching methods have been derived. These three primary approaches are known as the behaviorism, constructivism, and cognitivism learning theories. They have spawned additional approaches or extensions such as multiple intelligences, culturally responsive pedagogy, and critical pedagogy.

Oftentimes, these three learning theories are casually discussed in K–12 pedagogical conversations with little foundational understanding of their differences and implications. Moreover, these theories are even less frequently discussed and understood among college professors of various content areas. Consequently, professors are very versed in their respective content domains but have little theory to support how they teach it in the college classroom. There is a tacit, yet erroneous assumption that teaching is a natural power or extension that follows knowing.

As Fostnot explains, "Too often in the past, reforms in practice were not grounded in theory and thus took on a 'cookbook' faddism. We again run the risk of short-lived reform, or 'fuzzy-based' practice unless educators understand the theory."[1] Therefore, Part II discusses in historical order, the philosophical, theoretical, and practical implications and applications of the behaviorism, cognitivism, and constructivism learning theories.

Each theory has its unique insights and shortcomings. But one could argue that there is such a significant overlap of each of these theoretical understandings, trying to demarcate them into completely separate schools of thought is challenging. Professors should develop a personal pedagogical philosophy based upon these theories. Such an underpinning will help them establish practices for classroom design, instruction, assignments, and assessments.

BEHAVIORISM

Behaviorism, one of the earliest and probably most criticized of the three learning theories, approaches learning and knowing in a rather simple, yet sophisticated, fashion. To behaviorists, learning is simply a derivation of our innate brain responses to stimuli. Fundamentally, all people are in a constant and consistent state of rapidly analyzing what is being done *to* them and learning from how they react or respond.

During the early 1900s, before behaviorist principles came into vogue, the two eminent theories in psychology were structuralism and fundamentalism.[2] The structuralists focused on feelings and introspection while the functionalists studied the purpose of the brain's cognitive processes such as consciousness. Both theories had shortcomings: structuralism did not address contemporaneous scientific beliefs such as Darwin's work on evolution, and functionalism was limited to only very broad research implications.

John B. Watson, considered the developer of behaviorism, did not want psychology to concern itself with concepts such as the consciousness, because to him and many other scholars at the time, studying the consciousness was not sufficiently scientific. Watson preferred psychology to concern itself with brain functions that were measurable and observable. Therefore, to make the study of psychology more scientific he reasoned that human behavior would be worthy of their study, because it could be measured and observed and, therefore, could adequately explain how knowledge is transferred.

As Watson paved the way for behaviorism to take precedence in the field of psychology, Pavlov worked on measuring and observing behavior by creating and using a conditional model. Ivan Pavlov, the pioneer of classical conditioning, was interested in the idea that certain stimuli could illicit desired responses when reinforced with a reward, so that even when the reward was removed the desired response would still happen. He conditioned a dog to salivate when the animal heard the sound of a bell, and reinforced the behavior by providing a treat, which caused the dog to salivate. Eventually when the dog heard the bell, it salivated without seeing the treat.

Watson found Pavlov's work to be an exemplar for what he wanted behaviorism to represent. He believed that Pavlov's work could serve as the underlying structure for teaching and learning. Watson stated,

> Give me a dozen healthy infants, well-formed, and my own specified world to bring them up in and I'll guarantee to take any one at random and train him to become any type of specialist I might select—a doctor, lawyer, artist, merchant-chief and, yes, even into beggar-man and thief, regardless of his talents, penchants, tendencies, abilities, vocations and race of his ancestors.[3]

Watson understood learning as a process that occurs with environmental intervention. Therefore, behaviorism is not concerned so much with actual behaviors as it is environmental influences on individuals' responses. From this perspective, many theorists adopted this philosophical view of psychology, and it became the undercurrent of the behaviorist movement.

Learning According to Behaviorism

Edward L. Thorndike designed learning theories derived from behaviorism, which lasted for much of the first half of the twentieth century. Thorndike argued that learning was a result of the connections made in the experiences between the stimulus and the response. He believed that learning occurs through trial and error as individuals make connections through their experiences and subsequent consequences.

To garner his conclusions regarding how we learn, Thorndike observed the proclivity of cats when placed in conditioned environments, specifically environments where food and space were limited resources. In his observations he noticed,

> The starting point for the formation of any association in these cases, then, is the set of instinctive activities which are aroused when a cat feels discomfort in the box either because of confinement or a desire for food. This discomfort, plus the sense-impression of a surrounding, confining wall, expresses itself, prior to any experience, in squeezings, clawings, bitings, etc. From among these movements, one is selected by success. But this is the starting point only in the case of the first box experienced. After that the cat has associated with the feeling of confinement certain impulses which have led to success more than others and are thereby strengthened. A cat that has learned to

escape from A by clawing has, when put into C or G, a greater tendency to claw at things than it instinctively had at the start, and a less tendency to squeeze through holes. A very pleasant form of this decrease in instinctive impulses was noticed in the gradual cessation of howling and mewing.[4]

Conducting many behavioral studies on animals, Thorndike deduced they learned because they were motivated to obtain things like food and comfort. More specifically, their learning came about after they would choose a strategy to obtain what they needed and experience the outcome. Therefore, he reasoned that his observations of animals could be compared to that of human beings and how they learn, as well—that essentially all organisms would behave in the same way to illicit a desired outcome.

These research ideas were primarily based on experimental observations. However, the Law of Exercise and the Law of Effect also influenced these theories. The Law of Exercise includes the Law of Use and Disuse, and it refers to the incidence of a connection being strengthened or weakened due to the presence of a response to a stimulus or the lack thereof. In the college classroom, this law implies that a desired behavior from students is more likely to occur when a specific response by the professor is used to address the student when that desired behavior occurs. If there is not a specific response or association provided when specific behaviors occur, it is less likely that a significant neural connection will be made.

The Law of Effect refers to the emphasis on the consequence of a response. When a reward is received because of a particular response, the learning is strengthened; with a punishment, the learning is weakened. Therefore, with the understanding of this law, a professor could conclude that rewarding specific behavior is more likely to have a stronger learning association than that of providing a consequence. Under this theory, negative consequences essentially do not make as many neural connections in the brain for a student to lock the information into their long-term memories.

Burrhus Frederic (B. F.) Skinner had one of the earliest and one of the most profound influences on behaviorist learning paradigms. Skinner was able to use operant conditioning experiments with animals to understand how they are encouraged to respond contingent upon the type and frequency of the reinforcers. He used rats in his infamous "Skinner's Box" to explore their ability to learn how to press a lever that released food when all the environmental conditions were completely controlled.

Like speculations of Thorndike, some wondered how Skinner was able to reason animals and humans had cognitive similarities and, moreover, questioned his emphasis on behavior to explain human thinking. But he viewed animals and humans as fundamentally the same because they were both organisms. He also argued, when the later cognitivism movement gained popularity, that essentially everything we do as humans is a behavior—a response to something. To him, there was not a separation of the mind and the body because as organisms, every internal component was wired to react together in response to never-ending stimuli. Skinner stated,

> Cognitive psychologists like to say that "the mind is what the brain does," but surely the rest of the body plays a part. The mind is what the body does. It is what the person does. In other words, it is behavior, and that is what behaviorists have been saying for more than half a century.[5]

Essentially, our minds and consciousness are fundamentally our bodies reacting to everything. He went on to state,

Mathematicians and logicians have never given very consistent accounts of how they work, in part because they have tried to discover their "thought processes." If an artificial organism can be designed to do what logicians and mathematicians do, or even more than they have ever done, it will be the best evidence we have that intuitive mathematical and logical thinking is only following rules, no matter how obscure. And following a rule is behaving.[6]

Therefore, Skinner argued against the cognitive scientists and maintained his stance that emotions, consciousness, abstractions, and rationale are all, in essence, behavioral manifestations.

Through his early experiments in the 1930s, and well into his later research in the 1980s, educators realized the potential implications for the classroom regarding motivational strategies to keep students engaged in the learning process. He suggested that the teachers needed more effective training and preparation regarding the learning theories before entering the classroom. Using the support of his research-based evidence on high-frequency reinforcers, Skinner also suggested that teachers needed to provide very clear objectives with a plan, and to introduce positive reinforcement at high intervals.[7]

Concerning American education, Skinner vehemently addressed the shift from behaviorism to cognitivism in his article "The Shame of American Education."[8] As a result of the 1957 Russian-launched satellite—Sputnik—leaders in the United States began to shift their education priorities. The nation's leaders were suddenly concerned with the fact that the country was no longer the best in scientific and technological advances.[9]

Consequently, the priorities of US education were transferred to more scientific and technological courses. Thus, courses that promoted creativity and critical thinking such as art and social studies were reduced or eliminated altogether. Standardized assessments became the new way of testing students' abilities to process, punishment for lack of success in school was encouraged, and behaviorists' ideals began to fade out as cognitive ones took precedence. Consequently, Skinner's theories were denounced and replaced.

However, Skinner countered behaviorists naysayers by proclaiming that technology changed the way they viewed learning and was the reason for the shift away from his behaviorist models. He said, "Sensation and perception are reduced to input; learning and memory to the processing, storage, and retrieval of information; and action to output."[10] Skinner went on to add, "To say that students process information is to use a double metaphor, and how they process information is still the old question of how they learn."[11] He emphasized that even if the US priority was to be more internationally competitive, behaviorist principles in the classroom were more critical than ever.

Implications of Behaviorism in the College Classroom

In a purely behaviorist classroom, the professor takes the responsibility for teaching, and the student is the learner. The instructor establishes the goals and objectives, the pedagogical instruction, the assignments, and the assessments. It's a teacher-directed classroom environment. As such, the professor needs to make the objectives and instructional agenda clear to the students and to direct their learning. For example, pre-tests and post-tests, routine feedback, and the idea of mastering concepts before progressing to newer concepts are common practices in the behaviorist classroom.

Instruction based on the behaviorism foundation emphasizes eliciting specific responses from the learners.[12] Therefore, conditioning the students to learn the appropriate responses to specific stimuli is key. Additionally, creating an environment that houses the optimal stimulus and limits uncontrolled conditions is equally important. To enhance the learners' connections between desired responses to intentional stimulus, the behaviorist professor "frequently uses cues (to initially prompt the delivery of the response) and reinforcement (to strengthen correct responding in the presence of the target stimulus)."[13]

The repeated and strategic presentation of cues toward behavior, whether the behavior is the targeted behavior or not, can help the learner understand what their targeted behavior is. Instructionally, reward systems are common. What gets rewarded gets learned. In other words, the classroom environment needs to focus on and reward expected outcomes and behaviors and remove distractions to the achievement of those expected outcomes.

One approach used in classrooms is applied behavior analysis (ABA). ABA is a behavior-detailed modification made to enhance social and academic skills among students. It's a preventative approach that involves adjusting the environment along with positive reinforcement to illicit positive and appropriate behaviors. In other words, "Rather than focusing only on changing the student, intervention is directed at changing the environment. . . . Specifically, variables in the environment that trigger undesirable behavior are removed while environmental variables linked to desirable behavior are amplified."[14] For example, a professor might change the spacing of the classroom desks to allow for more face-to-face discussions to occur and provide positively affirming statements that, in turn, encourage students to comfortably share their thoughts.

As such, because the environment is something that can be controlled to a great degree by the professor, knowing what the desired behavioral outcomes are before teaching a lesson can help guide the learning approach. For example, if the desired outcome is to have the majority of the students actively engage in a class discussion, considering variables in the environment such as prior knowledge, seating arrangements, and safety would be advantageous. Likewise, students benefit when they understand at the outset of the lesson the objectives of the day and the plan to achieve them. A simple agenda or outline listed on the board as students enter the classroom can be most helpful. This then becomes a reference point throughout the lesson.

COGNITIVISM

Cognitivism was generated in response to the limits of behaviorism, which largely emphasized stimuli and response with little regard to conceptualizations and "how mental processes work."[15] Some psychologists—Piaget among them—argued that the behaviorists essentially simplified human cognition and that the theory was limited because it did not consider the complexities of the brain and its vast reactions to the environment.[16]

This theory is sometimes mistaken for constructivism, because like constructivism it considers the brain's ability to learn abstractly. However, cognitivism is unique from constructivism as this theory is more concerned with the computational components of learning. To cognitivist theorists, the brain is thought of as a computer that essentially processes information for knowledge absorption and not necessarily as a reaction to a stimulus or constructed influences. Conceptually, therefore, it resides between behaviorism and constructivism.

In the 1920s, Edward Chase Tolman challenged behaviorism by indicating that only thinking about the stimuli and response was "inadequate." He was concerned with the unpredictability of human nature, and the human reactions that were not observable. He theorized that there is a distinct difference between instinct and purpose, and that behaviorism did not account for the purposeful interior adjustment that people make in reaction to stimuli, and the variations of these reactions. Tolman posited that there may be more to our reactions to stimulus—that there may also exist thoughts and choices. To explain his curiosities, he gave the following example:

> Imagine a man trapped in a burning hotel. He may rush madly about in the same blind fashion as does the cat in the cage. If so, his behavior and that of the cat would seem to be identical. It may happen, however, that instead of this rushing blind feeling he stops to think. If such be the case, he does not attack all the exits of his trap indiscriminately, but only some which is apparently suggested to him by his "thought."[17]

Tolman continued,

> What, now, we may ask, is this thought and when and why does it occur? It will be remembered that in the initial statement of our program we declared that it was an objective, behavioristic account rather than an internal subjective one that we should aim to achieve; that we were interested not in how purposes felt, but in how they worked. Can we, now, shift our point of view and begin to talk about apparently internal subjective things such as thoughts? My answer is that thoughts, or at least the kind of thought with which we are concerned, can be conceived from an objective point of view as consisting in internal presentations to the organism (on a basis of memory and association) of stimuli not actually present but which would be present, if some hypothesized action were carried out.[18]

Thus, Tolman challenged the notion that human behavior was based on conditioning and predictability. He was essentially arguing, through numerous illustrative observations and examples, that humans learn through and act through considerations and hypothesized stimulus. In other words, we react because of what we know *may* happen. Essentially, we react with purpose.

Yilmaz concluded that, by the 1950s, the cognitivists understood:

1. Learning as an active process involving the acquisition or reorganization of the cognitive structures through which humans process and store information.
2. The learner as an active participant in the process of knowledge acquisition and integration.[19]

Generally speaking, it can be argued that Tolman's curiosities and experiments, based on his challenges of behaviorism, birthed cognitivism and gave rise to the well-known cognitive theories, such as those of Piaget, Vygotsky, and Brunner.

Learning According to Cognitivism

Jean Piaget has contributed much to the field of education in each of the major learning theories to some degree. However, particularly considerable of his contributions is his cognitive theory of equilibration. Learning, at its root, is an experience that essentially involves the brain receiving information or a stimulus and responding to it. However, unlike behaviorism, cognitivism takes to account other influencing factors. An interesting aspect regarding equilibration is the influence that one's numerous yet essential life experiences have on processing new information.

Genetics, parental guidance, nutrition, and the environment are examples of factors that may influence an individual's ability to process new content. Piaget explained this notion as equilibration. Equilibration is the process of a person receiving knowledge and then altering or adjusting it so that it makes sense to their own reality.[20] The learner decides to resist the information or accommodate it, contingent upon their background knowledge and how the information has been presented. Piaget claimed,

In the equilibration between the schemes of the subject, *A*, *B*, or *C*, etc., and the exterior objects, *A,*' *B,*' etc., the subject's actions, forecasts, judgements, and so forth, must not only possess certain characteristics *a,*' but the subject must also distinguish these characteristics from different characteristics, x, y, etc., considered as *non-a.*' Likewise, in order to use, judge, or classify *A'* with characteristics *a,*' we must turn to the scheme *A* and not to others considered *non-A*. It is evident therefore that only term, in extension as in comprehension, is opposed to any others, which infers process as many negations as affirmations; this relationship can remain implicit, but it often requires a more or less systematic delineation.[21]

Here, Piaget was essentially stating that humans, as learners, have a drive to achieve stability, and that new knowledge will be perceived in a way that relates to the learner. Therefore, if the learner has the capacity to respond and receive information as it relates to their own self-identities, it is important to encourage the growth of students as critical thinkers who actively think through their learning to more effectively consider how they sort new information as it is received.

One's ability to take in new knowledge and assess what he or she knows about it is metacognition. Piaget described metacognition as a cognitive developmental process that involves features such as environmental experiences and the need to assimilate and accommodate information to make sense of reality.[22]

Piaget is also well known for his four stages of cognitive development, which typically progress as a person ages. The four stages are sensorimotor, preoperational, concrete operational, and formal operational. He developed these stages through observational analysis.[23] His findings were significant in understanding how a child's ability to process information should be scaffolded. As a child grows, their ability to think becomes more abstract, and their ability to think about what they know and don't know, becomes more apparent to them.

This notion is not only significant to K–12 teachers. It's important for college professors as well, since many of our students essentially arrive at college as individuals who have not fully developed cognitively. Some of them are still teenagers Additionally, Piaget's formal operational stage is one that continues well into adulthood as individuals continue to learn to negotiate their everyday experiences.

Inner speech is an extension of Piaget's ideas of metacognition and equilibration. It involves the ability of an individual to self-regulate their thoughts when solving a problem or completing a task.[24] This complex process allows the learner to essentially talk themselves through problem-solving by reaching into the schemas of information they have compiled over their lives, sifting through it, and making new connections to generate solutions. Inner speech is incredibly significant to learning because the student can learn to self-regulate their mental processing.

Multiple Intelligences

The multiple intelligence theory is a very relevant extension of the cognitive approach, especially in the context of adult learners. Sadly, a number of our students unfortunately come to us with unfounded anxiety as they more than likely were indoctrinated with educational beliefs that there are only a couple types of "smart." Therefore, their overall sense of self—their self-efficacy—regarding what they can successfully do as college learners has already started off on the wrong foot.

Historically, North American education has been approached with an understanding that logistical (mathematical) intelligence and linguistic (language arts) intelligence were and still are essentially the most valuable types of intellect—and to an extent that they are the only types of intellect.[25] This is made inherently obvious by the extreme emphasis placed on standardized tests, because these overwhelmingly prioritize reading, writing, and math skills.

Howard Gardner, a cognitive psychologist, argued that this overemphasis on math and language arts was related to the creation of the IQ test. This test was primarily used to screen military soldiers when it was first designed. But eventually it took preeminence in the mainstream education system, as well, and became the universal marker of intelligence.

However, despite the long-lasting impact of the IQ test, Gardner argued that intelligence is incredibly subjective.[26] It is much more diverse than a simple funneling of two content areas. In other words, intelligence is more than only math and language arts. Therefore, students cannot be fully seen as intellectuals if we only consider those two types of knowledge.[27]

As such, Gardner proposed that there are many types of intelligences, seven in particular. The seven intelligences that Gardner suggested were: logistic, linguistic, spatial, naturalistic, kinesthetic, interpersonal, and intrapersonal. Gardner also argued that culturally, depending on what a given society values, these seven intelligences could vary. By focusing on these various types of intelligences, educators could view their students through a polysensitive lens. All students essentially possess intellectual strengths but in various and equally valuable modalities. This insight is essential to both instruction and assessment.

The typical approach to instruction has focused on using logistical and linguistical emphasis. Therefore, classrooms were and are mostly taught using verbal directives and puzzle types of activities. Furthermore, statistical data from multiple choice types of assessments (tests that only require objective responses) were chiefly used to assess and diagnose learners' abilities.

With this in mind, the implications for considering the multiple intelligences of students in a college or university course would be very beneficial. Many students may not realize they have a unique combination of intelligences.[28] Moreover, they may have never received validation for the types of intelligences in which they had heightened abilities due to their cultural background and experiences.

Therefore, offering a variety of instructional approaches can ensure that all students have opportune times to show what they know. Activities that involve discussions, debates, speeches, drama performances, visual creations, exploring the outside environment, creating music and poems, and solving problems with a variety of solutions are examples of how a professor could teach with the multiple intelligences in mind.

Additionally, providing students with a means to determine what their intellectual strengths and weaknesses are, is important as well. The point here is that educators should not just cater to students' conventional intellectual abilities. Our goal is to help them grow as well-rounded learners while, at the same time, they are empowered with their natural intelligence.[29]

Culturally Responsive Learning

Culturally responsive teaching is an extension of cognitivism. It flows from the understanding of how the brain is essentially hard-wired to think due to genetically passed down cultural dispositions as well as cultural experiences that are unique and consistent to each learner.

The word "culture" derives from "coulter," which is a plow used for farming or cultivation.[30] Raymond Williams stated that culture is simply an ordinary distinguisher of individuals. By this, he meant that culture is in everyone. Therefore, it can be devastating to limit culture to only the intellectual and upper classes.[31] Yet, that is how cultural capital came into existence; the idea arose that some cultures deserved to be *legitimate* ways of being, while others were expected to follow their lead. For instance, Ferrare and Apple wrote:

Culture then is what is found in the more pristine appreciations and values of those above the rest of us. Those lower can be taught such appreciations, but it is very hard and at times expensive work on the part of those who seek to impart this to society's Others and even harder work for those not yet worthy people who are to be taught such refined dispositions, values and appreciations.[32]

Culturally responsive educators recognize that cultural arbitraries move up and down the social hierarchical scale, facilitated by a very powerful and systematic institution: the school.[33] Professors, known as the intellectuals, carry the torch of defining appropriate culture by inculcating their students with the beliefs and values of the dominant cultural.[34] Educators then face the difficult choice of adopting and teaching the dominant doctrine or acknowledging the prosopography of the system and resisting it. It is difficult to accomplish this feat; however, to resist reproduction, one would have to go against the masses that work to legitimize it.

The task of reproducing dominance is an immense power struggle because people are already ingrained and programmed to see individuals for their perceived cultural capital.[35] Therefore, as a response to the oftentimes belittlement of certain cultures, culturally responsive teaching addresses the power structure that has decentered many students.[36] Additionally, it pioneers the notion learning can only truly occur when the content is culturally relevant. Thus, when the learning is culturally irrelevant, the brain may literally resist incoming information, triggering a flight, flight, or freeze response.

Giroux alludes to the notion that some educational institutions are reproducing dominant cultures and statuses through standardized approaches to the curriculum and a lack of critical thinking. Thus, some students may resist such a learning model as it essentially suggests there is a correct way to view the world, and that way only rewards those who represent that view.[37]

Implications of Cognitivism for the College Classroom

Cognitivists understand that learning is an active process and purposeful in intent. It demands the student is actively engaged as a critical thinker. A student's background, and the context of the learning environment and teacher support are central features in these classrooms. The instructor's role is to guide the learner and to provide the resources and necessary support for the student's journey.

In their journey, students seek stability, and they try to make sense of the world as it relates to them. Their learning is developmental and scaffolds upon previous learning—always seeking connections to other experiences. This necessitates reflection and introspection, processes of metacognition. As such, inner dialogue and self-regulation are critical practices and habits of students under the cognitive framework.

Instruction based on a cognitive foundation calls for professors to appeal to the students' preexisting schemata. In order for students to effectively accommodate new information, it is important that the professor is relatively aware of the students' background knowledge or allows students opportunities to sort through information in their long-term memories to make new connections to information in their working memories.

Methods for instruction should include culturally responsive approaches, visualizations of the new concepts, and information that immediately triggers the senses so the information can move its way through the working memory.[38] Moreover, professors are encouraged to use advanced graphic organizers and goal-setting strategies to help students organize information and develop cognitive practices. The key is that students can sustain equilibration as their brains are exposed to new information and actively and purposefully lock the information into new or preexisting schemata that can be called upon for future use as brain research suggests.

Therefore, professors need to be aware that students will have a variety of types of intelligences. So, a variety of instructional approaches that address those types of intelligences should be provided. Additionally, professors need to be aware of the cultural lens through which they view the content, and the life experiences of their students might be different, but just as valid.

CONSTRUCTIVISM

The third foundational and most influential learning theory is constructivism. Constructivism is a theoretical view of learning that is concerned with how knowledge is created through meaningful practices of the learner.[39] In response to the cognitivist movement, some learning theorists began to argue that principles of cognitivism were inadequate as they still did not fully address the whole picture of how we learn. For example, Greeno has argued that the following cognitivist assumptions were unfounded.

1. The locus of thinking is assumed to be in an individual's mind, rather than in interaction between an agent and a physical and social situation.
2. Processes of thinking and learning are assumed to be uniform across persons' situations. Different individuals are more or less capable of critical or creative thinking, and different situations are more or less conducive to learning and thinking, but the activities of thinking and learning are assumed to have approximately the same character wherever and in whomever they occur.
3. Resources for thinking are assumed to be knowledge and skills that are built up from simple components, especially through instruction in school, rather than general conceptual capabilities that children may have as a result of their everyday experience or native endowment.[40]

Constructivists, like many of the other learning theorists, argued that their approach to understanding of how one thinks was the most comprehensive. Additionally, constructivists believed that their concept of learning was not technically a learning theory, it was an epistemology. They studied how one comes to know information and were concerned more with the variety of types of knowledge and how individually all our learning processes are so extraordinarily unique that collecting empirical data to make their assumptions theoretical would be contrary to that idea.

Constructivists essentially view knowledge as a construction of one's reality and "no one version should be assumed to be more correct than any other."[41] In other words, cognitive processes are not just happening in each of our minds, they are happening in the context of where and how the information is transferred.

Learning According to Constructivism

Under the umbrella of constructivism, there are three distinct perspectives: exogenous, endogenous, and dialectical. The exogenous perspective is the assumption that the acquisition of knowledge represents one's understanding of their outside world. Therefore, an individual's obtained knowledge is as accurate as their representation of their actual reality. The endogenous perspective is the assumption that new knowledge generates from old acquired knowledge and is not always a reflection of the outside world. Finally, the dialectical perspective is the assumption that new knowledge is acquired through the mental negotiations of one's social interactions and the outside world.

Learning, to the constructivists, is more than listening passively at a desk within the four walls of a classroom. The teacher is responsible to facilitate learning, not to force their knowledge upon others. "The traditional hierarchy of teacher as the autocratic knower, and learner as the unknowing, controlled subject studying and practicing what the teacher knows, begins to dissipate as teachers assume more of a facilitator's role and learners take on more ownership of the ideas," according to Fostnot.[42]

This epistemological understanding proclaims that learning can and should happen everywhere and in every way. Learners should be directly involved with their learning by collecting information, observing, doing hands-on activities, and socializing to bridge their own unique understandings of concepts. Moreover, learning can occur virtually anywhere, such as the football field, a bus, the front yard of the school, the hallway, or an apprenticeship.

Because constructivist approaches in education were innovative, these views became known as the Progressive Education Movement. From this movement, there were, and continue to be, many prominent philosophers who have contributed to the perspectives of constructivism. Booker T. Washington, John Dewey, and Lev Vygotsky were among the most notable.

In 1881, Booker T. Washington began working as a headmaster in the newly founded Tuskegee Institute in Tuskegee, Alabama. The school was approved to operate as an African American training school. Washington, who had experience working in industry for a military officer, had an affinity for education principles that valued an industrial approach.

Washington created a curriculum for Tuskegee that called for the students to use their prior experiences to enhance their knowledge. He based the curriculum agenda on the students' social and occupational community needs. Therefore, Washington's curriculum infused student learning in the field with real-life examples. As a matter of fact, some of the Tuskegee students were responsible for building many of the institution's buildings during university expansion. Those students solved problems, thought critically, and communicated with one other to build stable structures on the campus. Washington believed the curriculum should embrace the students' lives. He stated, for example,

> In English composition it must be remembered that the problem of finding something to write about should be no problem at Tuskegee. The student's experience is full of impressions and ideas and inquiries which the very unusual environment flings at him every moment. Let him talk and write about the things he sees and handles and knows about and is interested in. Let him express his personal experience, the way the things he sees and does actually appeal to him as an individual.[43]

Washington argued that learning occurs when individuals address and negotiate their realities by *doing* and communicating. Additionally, Washington understood that words and theories were abstract ideas, and the only way to make them meaningful and traverse through the learner's mind into concrete ideas was to personally experience them. In other words, for a learner to adequately absorb a new concept, they must actually experience that concept in the real world through events such as constructive projects, field trips, and exploratory sensory activities.

Furthermore, to engage a learner and facilitate their absorption of new knowledge, social opportunities are essential. Appealing to learners' individual senses, their emotions, and their desire to effectively express themselves would facilitate their learning. Therefore, a teacher that teaches with only abstractions has created an "unnatural learning environment."[44] Learning is optimal in real-life settings with concrete examples.

At the time, African Americans were faced with the task of building and essentially creating their own communities and productive lives post–Civil War. Therefore, deciphering how to successfully do this was a popular topic of discussion among many prominent African American theorists. Washington's curricular approach was infamous because it was relatively controversial at the time. His educational concepts received both tremendous support and criticism. However, arguably, his methods were the predecessors to learning philosophers such as John Dewey. Furthermore, Washington's learning approaches remain popular at universities today. Many institutions offer vocational training and emphasize learning by students constructing their own knowledge.

It was during this progressive movement when the eminent John Dewey was born. This was an era where education was centered within the context of multiple social complexities; Dewey made significant contributions to what became known as constructivism. While obtaining his philosophy degree at Johns Hopkins University, Dewey was exposed to the seminar method. This method of learning using inquiry and discussion propelled his future ideas on the process of learning whereby students took more of an active role in their educational experiences, goal setting, and social interactions.

Dewey published many books on learning theory receiving international attention. One of his most prominent contributions to education and progressive education in particular, was his notion of experimentalism. Essentially, Dewey proposed that Western philosophies that emphasized the idea of separating the mind and body—cognitivism, for example, viewed learning as a search for universal truth—were based on fallacious assumptions. He argued that learning is endless and not concerned with finding a certain truth or universal understanding but, rather, about experimenting and experiencing. Therefore, Dewey viewed the process of learning as a whole mind and body experience that encompassed the human experience of imperfection.[45]

Due to his pragmatic philosophy, Dewey was concerned with the value of human experience in a constantly changing world. Contrary to philosophers such as Plato, who had fundamentally developed many Western approaches to education, Dewey wanted to emphasize learning as an exploration that did not ignore change or seek perfection. He emphasized that real life, with both its adversities and promotions, needed to constantly be reflected and expounded upon to solve issues not in search of a perfect truth, but for the sake of explaining our honest human experiences.

Like Washington, Vygotsky also emphasized communication as a primary component for learning. Complex conversations are necessary for students to exchange and reflect upon each other's differences and using their inner speech to understand their own self-identities within these exchanges. These conversations are pivotal in teaching tolerance and deflecting conformity.[46] Therefore, to Vygotsky, learning hinged on social inquiry and interactions. His theories of social constructivism focused on the importance of learning through the interaction and exchange of information with both peers and the instructor.[47]

Vygotsky also advocated for educators to be cognizant of their students' zone of proximal development, or ZPD. Vygotsky explained ZPD as a process of the teacher acting as a facilitator, by meeting the student where they are cognitively and introducing new concepts that the student can process through self-regulation to learn new ideas. Exposing students to concepts that are too abstract for their ZPD is ineffective teaching.

Margaret Gredler warns that professors need to resist pressures to meet imposed standards, locking them into upholding only a standardized ZPD.[48] In this vein, instruction is too often offered in a one-size-fits-all fashion, and students are expected to fit in or they will fall through the cracks. However, when instruction approaches the student in a method that considers what they already know, and their own unique capabilities, learning can be much more successful.

Michelangelo had the heart of a constructivist. He was asked how he could create such beautiful and life-like marble statues. He replied that the figure was already there; he only released it.

Critical Theory and Critical Pedagogy

Critical pedagogy is an extension of critical theory but also arguably an extension of constructivism. Fundamentally, critical theorists dissect systems and discourse by looking to find links to the suppression of an individual's true nature. For example, Tracy details how a critical theorist would have a unique response to the popular philosophical question,

> "If a tree falls in the woods and there is no one there to hear it, did it really make a sound?" The critical theorist might answer, "Well, why did the tree have to fall in the first place? Who cut it down? How might we shed light on the problem of deforestation?"[49]

The critical paradigm largely challenges notions upheld by European philosophers by acknowledging that their dominance is a cultural arbitrary inculcated on individuals of American society as themes of legitimacy. Lichtman states,

> Perhaps the most characteristic tenet of postmodern critical work is that everything that European philosophy and science has held to be fundamentally true at an abstract or programmatic level is in fact a contingent, historically specific cultural construction, which has often served the covert function of empowering members of a dominant social caste at the expense of others.[50]

Therefore, critical pedagogy would be used by those professors who want to promote societal change by resisting the teachings of domination and perpetuating the betterment of certain groups of students.[51] In other words, to the critical pedagogue, everyone's cultural background should be considered as primary aspects of the curriculum, not just little highlights here or there for the sake of learning to address direct societal concerns.[52]

In a system that has traditionally and actively suppressed the identities of unique individuals in search of achieving assimilation,[53] features such as race, gender identity, immigration, and socioeconomic status must be considered to make students' learning meaningful and foster their development as agents of change.[54] Additionally, the professor operating from a critical learning approach strives to address human rights through their curriculum and instruction because they find it fundamental to the learning process. As Canlas, Argenal, and Bajaj explain:

> First, students-whether operating from social locations of privilege or marginalization-must be able to feel human in the learning process. Through identifying their personal relationships to ideas of rights, dignity, and empathy, students can explore how their rights and those of others have been fulfilled or violated. Second, for all students but especially for those who occupy the margins, it is important that they see themselves in the curriculum and see examples of people from their backgrounds as agents of individual or collective change.[55]

Critical pedagogues work to resist societal status quo by encouraging critical inquiry and individuality. Thus, critical inquiry, the idea of questioning information to transform and accept it by taking a more critical view of society, is emphasized in instruction to encourage students to dig deeper into meanings and how they affect them.

Implications of Constructivism for the College Classroom

The constructivist classroom provides for a balance of mind and body experiences and interactions. It encourages experimenting and experiencing the learning context. Communication is a central feature in a constructivist classroom. Students interact with one another and with their environment in a shared social construct. The teacher aides or facilitates both complex group dynamic conversations and individual student self-regulation.

The constructivist professor encourages creativity through social learning. They encourage students to think critically by asking questions that promote higher order thinking skills instead of promoting their own opinions and beliefs upon the students.[56] The foundation of learning is based on the idea that every experience *is* learning. No matter how minute or trivial the constant influx of billions of bytes of information consumed by our brains may seem, our overall experiences are essential to the constructivist approach.

In many present-day college classrooms, creativity and constructive activities take the back burner for militaristic styles of learning. Students are typically expected to take orders and fall in line instead of speaking up and using differentiation as empowerment. As the achievement gap, standardized testing, and conformity have become the norm of American education, creative classes that highlight freshness and uniqueness such as the arts have been diminished.

However, research suggest that when students are having fun while learning and exploring concepts through socialization and discovery, their learning is strengthened.[57] Creative expression is the process of both metacognition and equilibration. It is learning in a pure sense as it allows the individual to address aspects of society and how they fit in it.

As Dewey explained, learning is not only about discovering universal truths, it's about experiencing concepts and *personally* engaging with the unknown to make meaningful discoveries. So, taking students on trips, having them work in groups, creating moments that call for investigation, allowing them to actually build things related to the content, and negotiating the curriculum as needs change and student concerns arise, are example strategies of the constructivist approach.

Therefore, the constructivist approach in the college classroom espoused by Booker T. Washington and others implies that learning should involve students being actively responsible for what they learn, and teachers should guide the process by providing appropriately rigorous exercises.[58] In the words of Brooks and Brooks, "Robbing students of the opportunity to discern for themselves importance from trivia can evoke the conditions of a well-managed classroom at the expense of a transformation-seeking classroom."[59]

Thus, foundational rules and concepts should be conveyed to students, but in methods that allow for exploration, self-discovery, and creation. For example, the professor must be aware of the conventional cultural norm within which their content is embedded. They and their students need to critically examine these norms and explore other views that may challenge and even strengthen conventional wisdom.

SUMMARY

Part II briefly described the historical and theoretical nuances of the three major learning approaches: behaviorism, cognitivism, and constructivism. Each theory has distinct characteristics, but ultimately, there are significant congruencies among their principles as well.

Behaviorism, one of the earliest theories, maintained the idea that all organisms learn through behavior, because everything that we do can be defined as a reaction to something. In other words, everything that we do is a reaction to something that has been *done* to us. When motivators are introduced in strategic ways, targeted behaviors can be cultivated. Therefore, simply stated, behaviorists believe that with targeted and intentional conditioning, people can be conditioned to learn anything because of the neural connections made due to the patterns and predictability of the intentional conditioning.

In contrast, and essentially in opposition to behaviorism, the cognitivists understood learning as more than a trained reaction to stimulus, but instead as very complex processes of knowing. Cognitivists unearthed a significant counter to behaviorists by speculating upon our ability to reason when something has been done to us. Learning is more than reacting; it's purposeful and deliberate thinking and interaction.

So, for instance, if a man is trapped in a burning house, his reaction to that stimulus may not necessarily be to jump out of the nearest window, but to assess the multiple escape routes and rationally choose the best one. Thus, this theory contributed to what we know about learning, because it proposed the ability of students to accommodate new knowledge based on their previous experiences. Those experiences, depending on how impactful they were, essentially glean connections in extremely intricate webs to inform our individualized choices.

Last, constructivism emerged onto the educational landscape as a reaction to both behaviorism and cognitivism. Unlike its predecessor learning approaches, constructivism adopted multiple angles of understanding. Fundamentally, knowledge is not necessarily something that can be easily funneled or measured, but its acquisition is primarily contingent upon the needs of the learner and their ability to make meaning on their own.

Therefore, constructivism is broad in its implications, but by its very nature it emphasizes the importance of personalized and socialized experiences as students create solutions to their everyday problems. So, academically and philosophically speaking, these ideals continue to expand into many new sub-theories such as critical theory and culturally responsive pedagogy.

Now that the three major learning theories have been introduced and discussed, considerations of course approaches can be made. To plan a course's curriculum and its instructional methods, intentionally using one of the discussed learning theories or a combination of them is important. The ethos of the classroom and desired cognitive outcomes are hinged upon clear cut learning theories that are manifested from how a professor views knowledge and its acquisition. Therefore, in Part III, we overview representations of each major learning theory by providing useful content-specific strategies to use in a college classroom.

NOTES

1. Catherine Twomey Fostnot, *Constructivism: Theory, Perspectives, and Practice* (New York: Teachers College Press, 2005), 11.
2. Dale Schunk, *Learning Theories: An Educational Perspective* (New York: Pearson, 2012).
3. John B. Watson, "What the Nursery has to Say about Instincts," in Psychologies of 1925, edited by C. Murchison, 1–35. (Worcester, MA: Clark University Press, 1926).
4. Edward Thorndike, *Animal Intelligence: Experimental Studies* (New York: Macmillan, 1911), 36.
5. B. F. Skinner, "Whatever Happened to Psychology as the Science of Behavior?" *American Psychologist* 42, no. 8 (1987): 784.
6. Skinner, "Whatever Happened to Psychology as the Science of Behavior?" 784.
7. Skinner, "The Shame of American Education," *American Psychologist* 39, no. 9 (1984): 947–54.
8. Skinner, "The Shame of American Education," 947–54.
9. J. Spring, *Deculturalization and the Struggle for Equality* (New York: McGraw-Hill, 1997).
10. Skinner, "The Shame of American Education," 949.

11. Skinner, "The Shame of American Education," 949.

12. Peggy Ertmer and Timothy Newby, "Behaviorism, Cognitivism, Constructivism: Comparing Critical Features from an Instructional Design Perspective," *Performance Improvement Quarterly* 6, no. 4 (1993): 50–72.

13. Ertmer and Newby, "Behaviorism," 50.

14. Glen Dunlap, Lee Kern-Dunlap, and Jonathan Worcester, "ABA and Academic Instruction," *Focus on Autism and Other Developmental Disabilities* 16, no. 2 (2001): 130.

15. Kaya Yilmaz, "The Cognitive Perspective on Learning: Its Theoretical Underpinnings and Implications for Classroom Practices," Clearing House: A Journal of Educational Strategies, Issues and Ideas 84, no. 5 (2011): 205.

16. Jean Piaget, *The Development of Thought: Equilibration of Cognitive Structures* (Presses Universitaires de France, 1975).

17. Edward C. Tolman, "Instinct and Purpose," *Psychological Review* 27, no. 3 (1920): 229.

18. Tolman, "Instinct and Purpose," 229.

19. Yilmaz, "The Cognitive Perspective on Learning," 205.

20. Leonora Cohen and Younghee Kim, "Piaget's Equilibration Theory and the Young, Gifted Child: A Balancing Act," *Roeper Review* 21, no. 3 (1999), https://doi.org/10.1080/02783199909553962.

21. Piaget, *The Development of Thought*, 10.

22. Schunk, *Learning Theories*.

23. Emily Fox and Michelle Riconscente, "Metacognition and Self-Regulation in James, Piaget, and Vygotsky," *Educational Psychology Review* 20, no. 4 (2008): https://doi.org/10.1007/s10648-008-9079-2.

24. Andrea Zakin, "Metacognition and the Use of Inner Speech in Children's Thinking: A Tool Teachers Can Use," *Journal of Education and Human Development* 1, no. 2 (2007): https://doi.org/10.1037/0003-066X.34.10.906.

25. Toni Bailey, "Othered Forms of Knowledge: Combining Theories of Aristotle and Bourdieu to Explore Intellectual Capital in the Curriculum," *Curriculum and Teaching Dialogue* 24, nos. 1 and 2 (2022): 51–65.

26. Howard Gardner, *Multiple Intelligences* (New York: Basic Books, 1993).

27. Bailey, "Othered Forms of Knowledge.."

28. Laurie Materna, *Jump Start the Adult Learner: How to Engage and Motivate Adults Using Brain-Compatible Strategies* (New York: Corwin Press), 2007.

29. Materna, *Jump Start the Adult Learner*.

30. Joseph Ferrare and Michael Apple, "Field Theory and Educational Practice: Bourdieu and the Pedagogic Qualities of Local Field Positions in Educational Contexts," *Cambridge Journal of Education* 45, no. 1 (2015): 43–59.

31. Raymond Williams, *Culture and Society 1780–1950* (London, UK: Chatto and Windus, 1958).

32. Ferrare and Apple, "Field Theory and Educational Practice," 43.

33. Pierre Bourdieu, "Cultural Reproduction and Social Reproduction," in *Power and Ideology in Education*, edited by J. Karabel and A. Halsey, 487–511(New York: Oxford University Press, 1977).

34. Pierre Bourdieu and Jean Claude Passeron, *Reproduction in Education, Society, and Culture* (Thousand Oaks, CA: Sage, 1990).

35. Bourdieu, "Cultural Reproduction and Social Reproduction."

36. Zaretta Hammond, *Culturally Responsive Teaching and the Brain: Promoting Authentic Engagement and Rigor among Culturally and Linguistically Diverse Students* (New York: Corwin Press, 2015).

37. Henry Giroux, Theory and Resistance in Education: Towards a Pedagogy for the Opposition (Westport, CT: Bergin & Garvey, 2001).

38. Jane Ellis Ormrod and Brett Jones, *Essentials of Educational Psychology* (New York: Pearson, 2018).

39. James Applefield, Richard Huber, and Mahnaz Moallem, "Constructivism in Theory and Practice: Toward a Better Understanding," *High School Journal* 84, no. 2 (2001): 35–53.

40. James Greeno, "A Perspective on Thinking," *American Psychologist* 44, no. 2 (1989): 134.

41. Schunk, *Learning Theories*, 230.

42. Twomey Fostnot, *Constructivism*, 11.

43. Booker T. Washington, "Principal's Annual Report," unpublished manuscript, Tuskegee Institute, *BTW Papers, Library of Congress*, 1902.

44. Donald Generals Jr., "The Architect of Progressive Education: John Dewey or Booker T. Washington" (2002), 186; In National Association of African American Studies and National Association of Hispanic and Latino Studies: 2000 Literature Monograph Series. Proceedings (Education Section) (Houston, TX, February 2000), 21–26.

45. Gerald Gutek, *Historical and Philosophical Foundations of Education: A Biographical Introduction* (New York: Pearson, 2011).

46. William Pinar, *What Is Curriculum Theory?* (New York: Routledge, 2004).

47. Margaret Gredler, "Understanding Vygotsky for the Classroom: Is it too Late?" *Educational Psychology Review* 24, no. 1 (2012): 113–31.

48. Gredler, "Understanding Vygotsky for the Classroom."

49. Sarah J. Tracy, *Qualitative Research Methods* (West Sussex, UK: Wiley-Blackwell, 2013), 43.

50. Marylin Lichtman, *Qualitative Research in Education: A User's Guide*, third edition) (Thousand Oaks, CA: Sage, 2013), 114.

51. Paulo Freire, *Pedagogy of the Oppressed* (New York: Bloomsbury, 2000).

52. Brenda McMahon, "Putting the Elephant into the Refrigerator: Student Engagement, Critical Pedagogy and Antiracist Education," *McGill Journal of Education* 38, no. 2 (2003): 257–73.

53. Bailey, "Othered Forms of Knowledge."

54. Carl Grant and Melissa Gibson, "The Path of Social Justice: A Human Rights History of Social Justice Education *Equity and Excellence in Education* 46, no. 1 (2013): 81–99.

55. Melissa Canlas, Amy Argenal, and Monisha Bajaj, "Teaching Human Rights from Below: Towards solidarity, Resistance and Social Justice." *Radical Teacher* 103 (2015): 38–46.

56. Freire, *Pedagogy of the Oppressed*.

57. Jacqueline Brooks and Martin Brooks, "Becoming a Constructivist Teacher," in *Developing Minds: A Resource Book for Teaching Thinking*, edited by A. L. Costa, 150–57 (Alexandria, VA: ASCD, 2001).

58. Gredler, "Understanding Vygotsky for the Classroom."

59. Jacqueline Brooks and Martin Brooks, "Becoming a Constructivist Teacher," section 1.

Part III

Implications and Applications

Professors are experts in their area of scholarship; however, such expertise does not automatically make one an excellent teacher. It also takes expert knowledge in pedagogy. In a seminal research study sponsored by the National Research Council we learned:

> Pedagogical content knowledge is different from knowledge of general teaching methods. Expert teachers know the structure of their disciplines, and this knowledge provides them with cognitive roadmaps that guide the assignments they give students, the assessments they use to gauge students' progress, and the questions they ask in the give and take of classroom life. In short, their knowledge of the discipline and their knowledge of pedagogy interact. But knowledge of the discipline structure does not in itself guide the teacher.[1]

After an analysis of how the brain learns, Part I concluded by providing some general implications for the college classroom. Part II provided a similar approach to describing implications after a description of contemporary teaching and learning theories. This section will now delve into more granular detail in describing brain and learning theory–compatible *implications* for professors in their curriculum development, their pedagogy, the types of assignments they give, and how they assess both their students' learning and the effectiveness of their own teaching. The last portion of Part III is devoted to *applications*—examples professors can use to recreate their own versions of lessons, assignments, and assessments.

The emerging implications are clear and specific. Much of what has been learned can be applied immediately to your own classrooms, and much of it supports the good teaching many professors are already doing. At the same time, these implications might also challenge some of what you have believed to be good teaching and should require some deep introspection and soul-searching. In describing the more authentic and natural classroom environment of the future, Dr. Robert Sylwester shared:

> Edelman's model of our brain . . . a junglelike brain might thrive best in a junglelike classroom that includes many sensory, cultural, and problem layers that are closely related to the real-world environment . . . that best stimulates the neural networks. . . . It's interesting to muse on such widely acclaimed developments as thematic curricula, cooperative learning, and portfolio assessment. All require more effort from teachers than do traditional forms of curriculum, instruction, and evaluation.[2]

Moreover, while we can learn a great deal from the various learning theories—all of which have specific, direct application to our classrooms from what we have learned of brain research and its implications for the classroom.[3] Part III will bring this brain research and learning theory[4] together for a cogent and robust model of teaching and learning, where students actively construct their own learning rather than passively receive it.

Just as we expect students to practice metacognition, or thinking about how they think, we must expect reflection of our own learning and of our own teaching. Knowing how we ourselves learn will help us appreciate how to connect our students to the discipline, but we must also acknowledge that not all of our students will approach learning the same way we do.

Sadly, our conventional class structures and teaching models are inflexible and often don't lend themselves to multiple teaching approaches or learning styles. This can then lead to a poorer quality of student learning. In the words of Jane Healy, "[i]t never occurred to us that the rigid system of which we were a part might be contributing to the problem."[5] One size—one approach—does not fit all students, or even all learning outcomes. More succinctly, different learning outcomes often need different teaching strategies.

Further, many of our teaching preferences have been influenced by cultural norms. For instance, in North America, the traditional educational approaches have been largely influenced by the industrial revolution, and international competitiveness through a Eurocentric lens. Consequently, many traditional approaches to teaching have involved cramming students with content for their memorization and immediate recitation on standardized exams—lower levels on Bloom's Taxonomy.

With a bit of reconsideration, and the support of brain research and learning theory, professors can make modest changes to their classroom instruction and perhaps have profound impact on their students. The implications and subsequent applications to follow range from the classroom environment to lesson design, from pedagogy to assignments, and from the assessment of students learning to that of our own teaching.

IMPLICATIONS

The Learning Environment

Once our brains feel safe to explore and try new things, they seek relevance to the information before them. Our brains then thrive on and seek challenging and novel material and learning opportunities. These are the types of attributes that best motivate learners, and as such, these cognitive opportunities use multiple regions of the brain to make stronger and lasting connections that can be drawn upon for future learning. In terms of how professors view their students, Ken Bain suggests the following:

> Highly effective teachers tend to reflect a strong trust in students. They usually believe that students want to learn, and they assume, until proven otherwise, that they can. They often display openness with students and may, from time to time, talk about their own intellectual journey, its ambitions, triumphs, frustrations, and failures, and encourage their students to be similarly reflective and candid. . . . Above all, they tend to treat students with what can only be called simple decency.[6]

What Bain is really suggesting is faculty mindset of student assets as opposed to a deficit model. Orthodox ideology would suggest students come to the classroom with deficits or gaps in their learning, and it is the job of the professor to fill in those gaps. Asset thinking focuses, rather, on the assets—the prior knowledge and experiences students bring to the classroom. Such a shift in ideology can have a profound impact on curriculum design and pedagogy.

The classroom can be an emotional place for students. In fact, college professors should carefully capitalize on emotional connections to their content. Robert Sylwester emphasizes,

"We know emotion is very important to the educative process because it drives attention, which drives learning and memory."[7] Laurie Materna elaborates: "Stronger emotions promote greater recall, while engaging too few emotions in the learning process tends to cause learners to quickly forget material unless it is rehearsed repeatedly."[8]

We have learned the human brain plays a central role in motivation. The brain is naturally motivated by a sense of curiosity, anticipation, and relevance.[9] Professors should take advantage of students' inherent tendency to want to find answers, to predict next steps, and for their search for meaning in what they do. Adult students especially want to take ownership for their own learning, and they need to be given the opportunity—the dignity to take ownership for their own struggle.[10] As such, the astute professor helps the student find why the topic is relevant to them. Jane Healy identifies three general principles of learner motivation:

> In order for any of us to be motivated for a particular task, three ingredients must be present: emotional connection, challenge, and payoff. The most effective payoff, however, takes the form of internal (intrinsic) satisfaction rather than external (extrinsic) reward.[11]

The National Academies of Sciences, Engineering, and Medicine explains, in part: "When learners believe they have control over their learning environment, they are more likely to take on challenges and persist with difficult tasks. Evidence suggests that the opportunity to make meaningful choices during instruction, even if they are small, can support autonomy, motivation, and ultimately, learning and achievement."[12]

The implications are critical for instructors. Before learning can take place, the students must feel safe and able to take cognitive risks. If their brains sense danger—or embarrassment, for example—their priority will not be on learning. One of the primary ways to help students to become motivated is to guide them to take their own control, to be self-motivated, and to create their own challenges. Payoff comes in the form of knowing they can succeed at the challenges they set for themselves for something they find intrinsically rewarding; they develop a sense of self-efficacy.

Such approaches are critical if we are to meet the foundational levels of Maslow's Needs Hierarchy. These first two critical levels show that if students are to learn, they must have their physiological, and safety and security needs met. Likewise, the students' feelings of belonging and being needed or valued are important considerations for professors. The classroom environment plays a central role in preparing the conditions for student learning, as such.

We further know the human brain is a social brain. Not only do students yearn for social connection but they also look for opportunities to contribute to others. Bransford and his colleagues explain: "Learners . . . are motivated when they see the usefulness of what they are learning and when they can use that information to do something that has an impact on others—especially their local community.[13] This insight again supports the hierarchical needs of student motivation explained by Maslow.

Jensen and McConchie provide a list of important Long-Term Motivational Strategies: "Autonomy, Student Empowerment, Success, Belonging, Social Status, and Challenge."[14] These contemporary notions support the attainment of the middle and upper levels of Maslow's original Needs Hierarchy for Motivation.[15] (See Figure 3.1.)

Again, each of us, students and professors alike, are motivated in ascending order by our most basic physiological needs, the need for safety and security, a need for social belonging and love, self-esteem, and ultimately self-actualization. Even Maslow's latter unpublished work proves to be prescient as he added: cognitive, aesthetic, and, finally, transcendent needs—the penultimate level. (See Figure 3.2.)

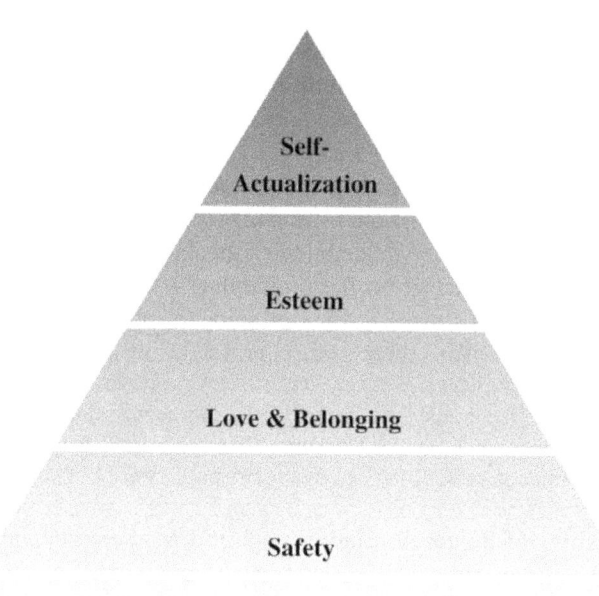

Figure 3.1 Maslow's Needs Hierarchy

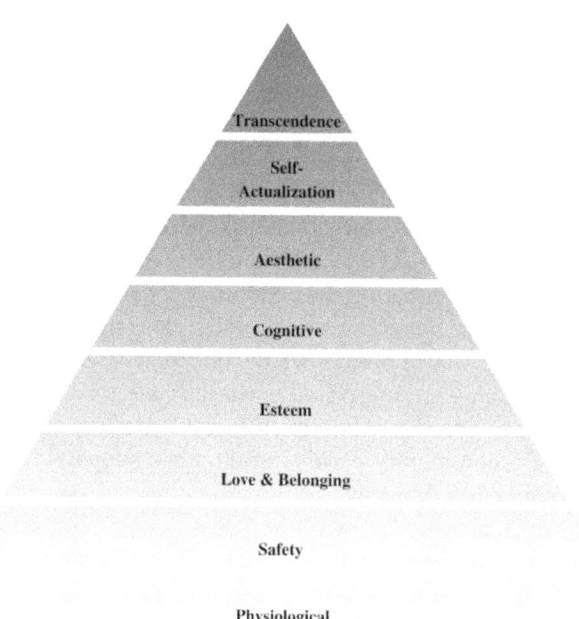

Figure 3.2 Maslow's Hierarchy of Needs with Transcendence

It's obvious that if a student is urgently hungry or thirsty, their minds will wander and won't be focused on the learning tasks at hand. Likewise, if they should feel bullied or harassed, their attention will drift. Similarly, when a student doesn't feel appreciated by the instructor or classmates, they will feel isolated and will be less able to attend to instruction. Should they feel disempowered, not cognitively feel up to the task, and feel they have little ability to meet the challenges ahead, they'll not likely be able to learn at an optimal level let alone to reach a state of self-actualization or even a sense of transcendence.

Our students need to have their most basic needs met. They need to feel safe, to belong socially, and to have a sense of self-efficacy. They need to feel they are making a difference. Keen professors will not only appreciate and embody these attributes, but they will deliberately set the tone in their classrooms and monitor for signs of concern from their students. These best professors will provide opportunities for students to work together, to take on ownership and responsibility for their own learning, and strive for an optimal level of challenge in their classrooms reaching into the community.

Instructors can help students take ownership for their own learning by teaching self-regulatory behavior. Students should set goals, plan ways to achieve them, and assess their progress.[16] As such, the students direct their own cognition and make adjustments as they learn. They practice metacognition. Professors help by accommodating student interests at appropriate cognitive levels.[17]

To put it another way—in terms of how the brain processes, all the sensory information that our brain receives from the outside world, with the exception of smell, enters the brain first through the brain stem, where the information is screened to determine if danger exists and whether a fight or flight response is warranted. If it is determined that the environment is safe, the brain continues to process the incoming information up through the middle brain's limbic system where emotions get triggered and where preceding memories are scanned for both relevance and again for safety. All of this happens instantly, and higher-order thinking has not even yet occurred.

Our best professors understand this and are certain to ensure their classrooms are a safe environment for learning to occur—a place for intellectual engagement and thinking to take place without a high level of stress.[18] These same professors understand the critical importance of emotional relevance to each student's learning experience and therefore create an environment where students feel comfortable yet sufficiently challenged to engage with and to explore the content at hand, always looking for ways to connect to other experiences as well as to their future ambitions. The brain seeks novelty and challenge.

The behaviorist instructor would adapt the classroom environment to support positive stimuli and negate distractions and seek to activate prior knowledge. The constructivist instructor would create a classroom of appropriate high challenge but low risk—one that encourages creativity and critical thinking through social interaction. The classroom environment sets the tone for teaching and learning—for the curriculum and for pedagogy.

Curriculum and Pedagogy

Once our classroom environment is prepared as an emotionally safe space filled with relevant experiences for challenging learning to take place, we can focus on cognition. In Part I, we learned how the brain develops, functions, and learns. While different regions of the brain play primary roles for different portions of learning and memory, they all work together holistically to function as the learning brain.[19] So, while there is some validity to left-brain and right-brain learners, some of these earlier suppositions were simply overstated. The whole brain works together and cannot function optimally in an isolated fashion.

Memories can be strengthened in the brain by using multiple approaches—kinesthetic, auditory, and visual, for example. Different regions of the brain are engaged, and existing neurons are strengthened when students commit something to memory by writing, speaking, and listening. Memories created this way are easier to recall when needed in the future. Repetition and continued practice further encourage neural growth,[20] and of course experience situated in an emotional context is more likely to drive the learning home.

The knowledge of how our brains learn has obvious implications for how we structure our classrooms, how we design our curriculum, and how we implement our pedagogy. For example, we need to create a pleasant classroom setting which encourages dynamic engagement with the content and social interaction along with opportunities to engage our multiple senses. Importantly, the brain thinks in terms of visual imagery and not in text as in our largely text-dependent curriculum.

Suzanne Wade and her colleagues discovered that college students were more interested and retained textbook information better when: the information was important, new, and valued; the information was unexpected; the text supported readers in making connections with prior knowledge or experience; the text contained imagery and descriptive language; and the author attempted to relate information to readers' background knowledge using, for example, comparisons and analogies.[21]

Professors can also use interactive lectures where they introduce a topic and students discuss how it can be applied in real-life settings or with their own experiences. Leamnson expresses, "Properly done, there are few more effective devices for learning than studying in small groups. . . . and study followed by individual reports would seem to provide optimal results."[22]

We all experience times when we are reading or listening to someone, and our minds begin to wander. We should take this as a signal to either consciously focus hard for a few more minutes, or to take a break, or to switch up tasks for a few moments. Richard Restak quotes golf coach Jim McLean: "Practice only as long as you can concentrate. Stop when you . . . lose focus. Short, focused practice sessions are often the most productive."[23] If we keep lecturing beyond the students' attention span, we're wasting our breath, and we're wasting learning opportunities. We simply need to switch up what we're doing in order to be more effective and productive. Sometimes we simply need to build in brain breaks for our students—breaks for only a couple of minutes.

Not all researchers will agree on the best way to reach learners, but they do agree on the necessity of using multiple approaches and through multiple senses. Colin Rose, for example stated that "learners remember 90 percent of what they see, hear, say, and do, as compared to only 20 percent of what they read, 30 percent of what they hear, 40 percent of what they see, 50 percent of what they say, and 60 percent of what they do."[24] The message is clear: use multiple instructional strategies and sensory modes where you can in order to afford your students the best opportunity to learn.

For optimal intellectual engagement, it is better to have our students become "note-makers" rather than "note-takers." Rather than passively taking notes, they need to engage and make sense of the material by creating notes in their own words. It is also beneficial for them to verbalize or discuss the notes that they make, which not only helps them to clarify their thinking but it also provides additional synaptic connections in the brain. As such, students will need help from their professors as how to actually make notes—how to take what they hear and read, and then put into their own words and connect them to their own experiences and context.

"The most effective teaching will be done by teachers who vary their approach, use different methods of instructing within the same class period, and never let their students get comfortable," according to Robert Leamnson.[25] This can be a matter of mixing mini-lectures, with discussion (small and large group), debate, visual aids, hands-on activity, writing, problem-solving—all with the intent to emotionally connect, to find relevance and meaning, and connection to the material. Such multiple approaches not only help to keep the students' attention but they also use multiple parts of their brains and are more likely to incorporate learning across various regions of the brain in a more dynamic fashion.

In an interesting study, researchers found that typing notes is less impactful on student writing than when students handwrite notes and put the notes in their own words.[26] The former is a more passive approach and doesn't necessarily invite cognitive engagement, while the latter is more assertive in nature, requiring student intellectual engagement.

One common element to all this previous discussion is that of time. It takes time to learn, and it takes time to teach. Students need to be given time to intellectually grapple with the content they are being taught. Time is needed for them to think, to write about, to discuss, to practice in project form. But they need time. Professors not only need to use time strategically in their instruction and their assignments but also in how they ask questions. They purposefully use wait time.

There are two forms of wait time. The first wait-time occurs when the professor asks the class a question. After they ask a question, they typically call on a single student for a response. The average amount of this wait time is an astonishing 1.5 seconds, at most. The student called upon has little time to reflect, to think, and to provide an answer.

Furthermore, all the other students are relieved to not have to provide an answer and can stop thinking. Instructors should experiment with their own wait time and give students more time to think. Likewise, they should consider strategies where all students need to respond, not just the one. For example, all students could be asked to write a response or to share with others. The idea is to get all students sufficient time to be challenged to think and to engage with the concepts.

The second wait time occurs after the student has provided their answer. All of us professors are prone to feel compelled to respond immediately. We acknowledge their answer with affirmation, negation, or some other nuanced retort. But the student is typically off the hook at this point. If we wait—if we don't respond immediately to their answer, the student will be searching inside to determine whether they were correct. They may choose to elaborate. In other words, they will be thinking. These two wait times intuitively make a great deal of sense to excellent professors. But the challenge to effectively implement them is more difficult than it might appear.

Once we have a firm understanding of the basic principles of how the brain learns, professors can re-examine their curriculum to determine how best to teach their content. Writing for the National Research Council, John Bransford and his colleagues stipulate:

> The fact that experts' knowledge is organized around important ideas or concepts suggests that curricula should also be organized in ways that lead to conceptual understanding. Many approaches to curriculum design make it difficult for students to organize knowledge meaningfully. Often there is only superficial coverage of facts before moving on to the next topic; there is little time to develop important, organizing ideas.[27]

A recurring theme in this book is that students create their own learning by active engagement, making personally meaningful relevance of the content, and practicing metacognition of their own learning. This is considered a learner-centered classroom.[28] However, students may have erroneous prior content or conceptual knowledge, or they may not have the intellectual tools required to navigate new material. The feedback needs to be specific and targeted.[29]

Hence, an intersection of a learner-centered approach with a knowledge-centered approach is necessary. Again, Bransford and his colleagues express: "Knowledge-centered environments also focus on the kinds of information and activities that help students develop an understanding of disciplines."[30] The best instructors walk the fine line of focusing on both the content and the knowledge, and on how to best reach individual students' learning.

Too often, the conventional curriculum is structured in isolation from other content and other disciplines. This makes it virtually impossible for students to see and understand the bigger unified whole, one that promotes integration for new meaning and understanding. Memorizing facts or concepts in isolation from context does not promote optimal learning. Such traditional approaches are teacher-based models of instruction. But more contemporary learning theories provide insights to mitigate these concerns. According to Bransford and his colleagues:

> An alternative . . . is to expose students to the major features of a subject domain as they arise naturally in problem situations. Activities can be structured so that students are able to explore, explain, extend, and evaluate their progress. Ideas are best introduced when students see a need or a reason for their use—this helps them see relevant uses of knowledge to make sense of what they are learning.[31]

Moreover, our traditional approaches to teaching and learning have provided a singular, often erroneous, perspective of how we identify giftedness, often through such measures as IQ and standardized tests. Michio Kaku is clear: IQ tests "actually give no definition of intelligence in the first place."[32] Such ways of identifying our best students frequently keep us from identifying creative and otherwise truly gifted and talented students.

According to Jane Healy, these other prodigious students prefer to: use more strategic than problem-solving approaches; seek patterns and relationships; connect concepts in knowledge webs; prefer complexity; are adventurous in their learning; and are self-disciplined in their academic pursuits.[33] These are the sorts of learning experiences that help all students, irrespective if they have been deemed as gifted, make sense of the content.

Finally, Healy implores teachers to be purposeful in their curriculum design and pedagogy. She asks that students be given opportunity to work together, and for self-evaluation to be routinely practiced. In particular, "A creative classroom is not an excuse for mayhem or disorganization. Master teachers who focus on creative enrichments carefully plan and evaluate each activity."[34]

According to Bransford and his colleagues:

> An alternative . . . is to expose students to the major features of a subject domain as they arise naturally in problem situations. Activities can be structured so that students are able to explore, explain, extend, and evaluate their progress. Ideas are best introduced when students see a need or a reason for their use—this helps them see relevant uses of knowledge to make sense of what they are learning.[35]

As professors begin their pedagogical role of engaging their students with the content, they need to be comfortable with their role not as a "sage on the stage" but more a "guide on the side," or an expert who helps students wrestle with the content, to scaffold off previous learning, and to connect with authentic and meaningful experiences. Such teaching and learning are not purely linear and concrete; they are dynamic, organic, and malleable, just like the human brain. Stephen Covey said some of his best lessons lived on the edge of chaos.[36] As such, these contemporary classrooms move from one dominated by teacher-centered instruction, to learner-centered or even learning-centered instruction.

We also need to reconsider the role and utility of conventional lectures. Lectures are good vehicles to get across material, especially factual, in a relatively short period of time. The model is based, however, on the belief that knowledge can be transmitted to and subsequently absorbed by the students. It's a passive approach to learning. Still, lectures can show students not only what content the professor believes to be most important to learn but also lecturers can show students what and how experts think.

Higher-order thinking and understanding of the material cannot be conveyed in the conventional manner,[37] however. Robert Leamnson suggests some alternative techniques to traditional lectures:

1. Dialogue with Students. Take the time each lesson to focus on dialogue with just a few students to monitor their understanding and progress, and to help them think deeply about new concepts.
2. The Interrupted Lecture. Shorter, or mini-lectures, are more effective than one prolonged lecture. A break between lectures provides students to recalibrate and to intellectually integrate what they've learned, perhaps through discussion or other activity.
3. Progress Report on an Assignment. Students can benefit immensely from 1:1 interaction with a professor before or after class to dive deep into a topic. This provides the students the opportunity to think deeply and engage in ways they might not otherwise, but it also provides the professor the opportunity to learn what the students know, as well as where their understanding is faulty.
4. Give Students a Chance to Instruct. When students are expected to teach their peers, they are forced to really study a topic—to understand it to a degree they might not otherwise as a passive recipient of a lecture. Such practices take time, of course, and the professor must monitor for accuracy and clarity.
5. Debate the Debatable. Giving students the opportunity to formulate a logical argument, to present their case, and in turn to listen to counter arguments has immense benefits. Like the previous techniques, this strategy requires active engagement and oversight by the professor, and it of course takes more time than a straightforward lecture.[38]

By stretching the learners' intellectual rubber bands, the professor can create cognitive dissonance. For instance, if a student believes X, but their actions are aligned with Y, there will be an obvious cognitive disconnect, and the student will naturally want to rid themselves of this angst. They may change their action or perhaps their belief from such an intellectual struggle. After all, adults do not want to be passive sponges; they desire the freedom of ownership and responsibility in their own learning and thinking. The classroom is an optimal place to explore, to challenge, and to be challenged.

Pulling the finer points of learning theory together, we know that learning is contextual and is most successful when prior learning is activated and used to scaffold new concepts. As such, professors need to work from students' existing knowledge and bring in long-term memory to help lay the foundation for new learning. It is helpful for students to use multiple senses when they approach new concepts and to find the content relevant to their lives.

ASSIGNMENTS

Assignments need to flow directly from the content objectives and extend from the corresponding instruction. In other words, professors begin with the end in mind—the goals and objectives for the unit. They then design lessons and instruction to reach those goals and objectives. The assignments should be natural extensions of this instruction. Since so much learning takes place outside the classroom, teachers need to take advantage of this time through their assignments to make them relevant and productive.

For the most part, there should be less reliance on simplistic traditional worksheets, with exceptions of lab sheets or study guides, for example. Again, Bloom's Taxonomy would serve as a perfect model to help the instructor gear assignments to varying levels of higher order thinking, always based on the goals and objectives of the content, of course. Opportunities for analysis, synthesis, evaluation, and creation should be considered.

This suggests that more authentic and reality-based assignments are optimal. Such assignments can be problem-based or community-based, but they need to be relevant to the students' lives, and the students need to see the relevance. In its 2018 report on *How People Learn II*, the National Academies of Science, Engineering, and Medicine noted, in part:[39]

> A number of studies suggest that situational interest can be a strong predictor of engagement, positive attitudes, and performance, including a study of students' essay writing[40] and other research.[41] These studies suggest the power of situational interest for engaging students in learning, which has implications for the design of project-based or problem-based learning.

Problem- or project-based assignments focus on process as opposed to learning outcomes. According to Barbara Condliffe and her colleagues, "The challenge should be one that drives students to grapple with central concepts and principles of a discipline and to develop constructive investigations that resemble projects adults might do outside of school."[42] Developmental portfolios are prime examples of authentic assignments that can most certainly be relevant and problem-based. Such developmental portfolios can exist within a course or even extend across a student's entire academic program or major.

Today's college classrooms enjoy an eclectic mix in the age of their students. While traditional students still occupy a majority of the seats, an increasing number of nontraditional and older adult students have entered degree programs. Adult students may very likely have different goals and life experiences than college students directly out of high school. For example, they may be looking for job promotions or career changes. Most likely they will know precisely what they will accomplish and will have established clear goals they wish to pursue. They are self-directed, and the astute professor will capitalize on this understanding.

Anyone who has served as an employer and hired workers understands the necessity of authentic experiences when looking for new employees. The conventional college transcript does not tell an employer much. In fact, employers don't use transcripts at the point of hire. They only use the transcripts for credential verification—an HR function. Frankly, the traditional transcript does not tell an employer anything too important. All students today take mostly the same courses and earn roughly the same grades. Transcripts don't serve the purpose of differentiating candidates. What sets the best potential employees apart from the rest?

Portfolios of authentic, real-life experiences can make the difference. Portfolios are tangible examples of work that students have actually completed. They focus on a project from start to finish, show development, problem-solving, and results. Most likely they cover the various levels of thinking and action of Bloom's Taxonomy. They show what a potential employee can actually do. This is where a professor's classroom can make the difference by helping the student take the abstract and conceptual and turn it into something tangible, relevant, and meaningful both to the student and to the employers and community.

Assessment

One of the most important responsibilities excellent instructors perform is the assessment of student learning and the effectiveness of their own teaching. According to the 2018 report by the National Academies of Sciences, Engineering, and Math, "Assessment is a critical tool for advancing and monitoring students' learning in school. When grounded in well-defined models of learning, assessment information can be used to identify and subsequently narrow the gap between current and desired levels of students' learning and performance."[43]

Broadly speaking, there are two forms of assessments—formative and summative. Formative is an ongoing assessment that is most likely quick, informal, and often not graded. It consists of a variety of techniques designed to see if students understand the material, or where errors of cognition are being made, before deciding to move forward or to reteach the content. By determining where students' thinking is faulty, the professor can point out the errors in understanding, adjust their instruction, and help the learners reconceptualize. Just like the best coaches adapt to their team, the best professors adapt their instruction to their students' needs.

Summative assessment is most often formal, graded, and summarizes learning at the end of a unit of instruction. Some summative assessments are high stakes. In these cases, a final grade can determine whether a student passes a course, or even graduates. Both types of assessment are central to education, but in the estimation of these authors, formative assessment is the most valuable. It is absolutely critical to keep in mind that all assessment should be used to provide feedback to the students about their learning and to the instructor about their teaching, not just a formal marking point.

Assessment is an opportunity for the professor to have a teachable moment—to review the answers after the test is handed back, for example. Everyone who has at one point been a student knows they have guessed on the answers to some questions. If the test results are never discussed, students will never know if they guessed correctly, or have the opportunity to learn the correct answer. This is a missed opportunity for professors and learners, alike. "The most important function of testing is not to provide a basis for grading. Rather, tests are an important educational tool . . . [for] corrective feedback."[44] The National Academies of Sciences, Engineering, and Medicine elaborates:

> Research suggests that feedback is most effective when it is focused on the task and learning targets; that is, detailed and narrative, not evaluative and graded; delivered in a way that is supportive and aligned with the learner's progress is delivered at a time when the learner can benefit from it; and delivered to a receptive learner who has the self-efficacy needed to respond.[45]

Memory is quite fallible, and people often make mistakes when they attempt to learn new material or to connect it to preexisting knowledge and experience. Metacognitive processes are very helpful in determining where errors may exist.

In addition, low-stakes formative writing exercises help to determine what students know and don't know, and these can provide learners with additional opportunities to think. Such writing prompts help students know what is important and what to explore, process, and learn about. It keeps them focused, gives them practice in writing for high-stakes assessments, helps them put concepts into their own words, and engages them in their own learning. Formative assessments also indicate to the learners what the instructors deem most important.

The use of high-stakes assessments should be limited. There is frequently a sense by employers that college students can't *do* anything other than take tests. When high-stakes assessment is required, since such high risk is involved, the accuracy of these tests is imperative. Forms of triangulation or multiple measures can help to mitigate some of these concerns. Grading rubrics (examples shared later) can help provide validity and reliability. Rubrics can also be useful tools to guide instruction and to help students know what is considered important by the professor. Often, the best professors will share grading rubrics with the students at the beginning of the learning segment, providing the learners with guideposts for success.

Authentic and performance-based assessments are also strategies that can help mitigate concerns of high-stakes tests. Such examples as case studies, scenarios, and real-life and

Figure 3.3 Bloom's Learning or Cognitive Taxonomy

community problems are good examples. (Again, samples are shared later.) Interrater reliability becomes an issue when grading authentic assessments, and even when using rubrics for that matter. Practice sessions for instructors are advised. Every seasoned professor knows that they could grade a paper one day and score it differently another day. This situation is exacerbated if multiple instructors are grading the students' work.

Finally, assessment needs to be purposefully built into the instruction, and it needs to become a part of our instructional routine. It needs to measure the quality of the students' learning and cognition. The old saw, "What gets assessed gets learned," could not be truer. For students preparing for exams, "cramming" is not effective. The brain needs time to process and to make connections. "The best way to prepare for a final exam is to mentally review the material periodically during the day, until the memory becomes part of your long-term memory."[46]

Still, not everything we teach or that the students do needs to be assessed or given a grade. Quite frankly, some things are just very difficult to assess—to measure. McKeachie and Svinicki bemoan, "Admittedly, it is more difficult to devise measures of complex, higher-level objectives."[47] A quick review of Bloom's Learning Taxonomy is warranted, again. (See figure 3.3.). Lower-level learning objectives on Bloom's Taxonomy are typically fairly easy to measure with factual kinds of examinations. The further one goes up the taxonomy however, the more difficult it is to measure and to be valid in the assessment. Instructors need to be careful when assigning grades and other high-stakes decisions based on ever-increasing concerns of measurement validity. (Examples will again be shared in the next portion of Part III.)

APPLICATIONS

Curriculum Map: Behaviorism

Step 1: Identify the desired behavior.

Step 2: Identify the college or university's mission statement.

Step 3: Identify the department/division/program objectives.

Step 4: Create course objectives that align with your desired behavior, college, or university's mission statement, and department/division/program objectives.

Step 5: Create an inclusive and equitable course content presentations and key assignments that align with the course objectives and include motivational factors and repetition.

Step 6: Assess the students.

Step 7: Reflect and revise.

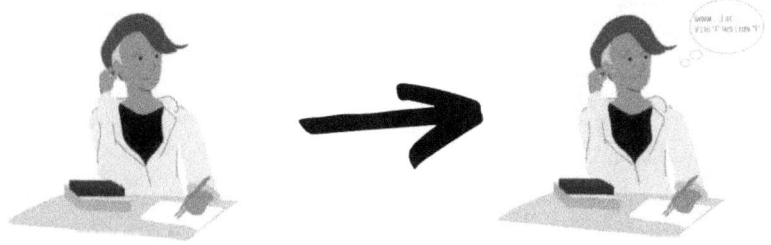

Strategies: Behaviorism

Teaching the Content	*Assignments*	*Assessments*
Create patterned practices for each course meeting that consistently upholds inclusivity and equity and provides immediate and frequent feedback • establish and uphold normed responses • prompt daily warm-up discussions • activate prior knowledge • infuse students' experiences • strategically design the physical space • routine class closings Provide immediate and frequent feedback Dynamic chunked lectures (No more than forty-five minutes at a time) or content may be taught in other consistent ways. Examples: case study analyses related to the content; student presentations; grouped student work; and role-play.	• journaling "the what, so what, now what?" • Socratic seminar discussions • case study analyses • jigsaw activities debates • research papers • presentations • projects (i.e., create a mock design, or a visual representation of a concept) • surveys data collection • portfolios graphic organizers (i.e., Venn diagrams, bubble maps, concept maps)	• formative quizzes • observations • written responses • discussions • games • summative presentations • portfolios • research essays • examinations • graphic organizers • critiques • speeches • debates projects Use a consistent feedback and grading system (fair and defined assignment relevant criteria).

The Key is Consistency

BEHAVIORISM: TEACHING THE CONTENT, EXAMPLE 1, THE THINKING MAP

- professor's desired behavior for students: using evidence to defend a stance during discussions
- student motivators: empowered voice
- positive reinforcer/the strategy: the thinking map (can be used during each course meeting as a warm-up activity)

Step 1: Routinely provide a provocative image related to the course content on the display board (or if teaching online, present the image as an upload or on a shared screen).

Step 2: Hand out a Thinking Map printout (or alternatively, have students draw the bubble map in their course notebook).

Step 3: Tell students to use course-related vocabulary words to describe different aspects of the image, using their own unique lens to draw such connections.

Step 4: Facilitate students in explaining their reasoning for their responses in a class discussion.

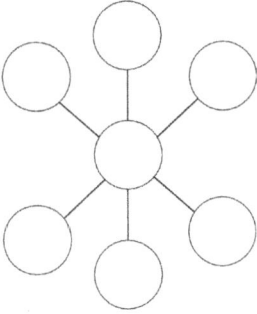

BEHAVIORISM: TEACHING THE CONTENT, EXAMPLE 2, THE DYNAMIC LECTURE

- professor's desired behavior for students: improved comprehension and memory of content
- student motivators: comprehension and self-confidence positive
- reinforcer/the strategy: the dynamic lecture

The Dynamic Lecture Sequence (Two-Hour Course Session)

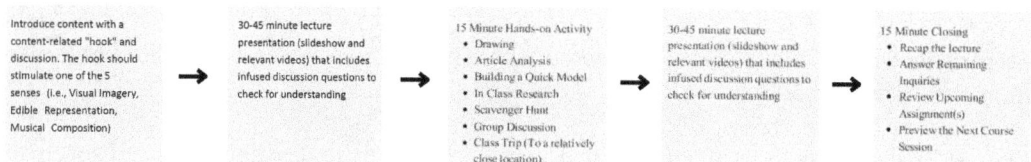

BEHAVIORISM: TEACHING THE CONTENT, EXAMPLE 3, THE THREE I'S ASSESSMENT REFLECTION

- professor's desired behavior for students: cultivate a growth mindset toward assessments
- student motivators: internal reflections and self-efficacy
- positive reinforcer/the strategy: the Three 'I's Assessment Reflection (can be used after formative or summative assessment)

The Three I's Assessment Reflection

Initial Reaction to Results

Provide one word that describes your initial reaction to your assessment results:

Item Analysis

Analyze each question. For the questions you answered correctly, address how you were able to gain success on those questions. For the questions you answered incorrectly, address if the incorrect responses were due to unpreparedness or misunderstanding.

Internalize

How can you continue the successes that you made? How can you improve upon *moments* of inaccuracy?

BEHAVIORISM: ASSIGNMENT EXAMPLE 1, STUDENT-LED CONTENT DISCUSSION

- professor's desired behavior for students: content transferability
- student motivators: capacity to lead
- positive reinforcer/the strategy: student-led content discussion

Student-Led Content Discussion:

Have each student lead a ten-minute class discussion and interaction about one of the theories covered in the recent readings.

Inform Students:

"Your job is to glean out relevant primary and secondary source documents and extract a few key writings to share with your peers for a class discussion. Try to find quality exemplars of the work . . . emphasizing the quality vs. quantity. Select several key paragraphs that demonstrate the thinking behind the theory. You may also want to consider its pros and cons. During your presentation, encourage a variety of opinions and engagement from your peers."

Scoring Criteria for the Presenters

- organization and preparation—ten points total
  - background research on the topic was evident; presenters stayed within the ten- to twelve-minute time limit
- leadership skills—knowledge level—ten points total
  - presenters gave a brief overview of the theory
  - presenters involved the class in deep explorations of the theory
  - presenters led the class in rich discussion questions about the theory tenets relevant to their professional practice
  - presenters helped their peers see connections to previous or future theoretical strands
- leadership skills—delivery level—five points total
  - presenters designed a quick activity to help their peers critically analyze the theory

BEHAVIORISM: ASSIGNMENT EXAMPLE 2, SOCRATIC SEMINAR

- professor's desired behavior for students: engaged sense of community
- student motivators: inclusivity, self-confidence, critical thinking positive
- reinforcer/the strategy: Socratic seminar

Routinely have students engage in Socratic seminars via discussion board posts or in class.

Inform the Students:

In your discussion post, propose at least two text-dependent questions related to the central ideas and themes of this week's readings (your questions can be from one text and/or both) to your classmates.

- Respond to at least two of your classmates' questions.
- In your response, include: your claim/response to the questions, supporting evidence (text, class, society at large), a possible counterclaim, and how you would refute it.
- Also, respond briefly to those who answered the questions you originally posted

BEHAVIORISM: ASSESSMENT EXAMPLE, DEMONSTRATION EXAMINATION

- professor's desired behavior for students: comprehensive understanding of content student motivators: course success
- positive reinforcer/the strategy: demonstration examination

Question Types	Holistic Assessment Rubric for Extended Response Portions		
multiple choice true/false figure/diagram drawing case study analyses questions	**Question#** grammar and spelling logical reasoning	**Points Possible**	**Explanation**

Curriculum Map: Cognitivism

Curriculum Map: Cognitivism

Step 1: Identify both the course outcomes and the students' prior knowledge

Step 2: Create scaffolded lectures and assignments that will connect to the students' prior knowledge and eventually facilitate their growth towards the course outcomes

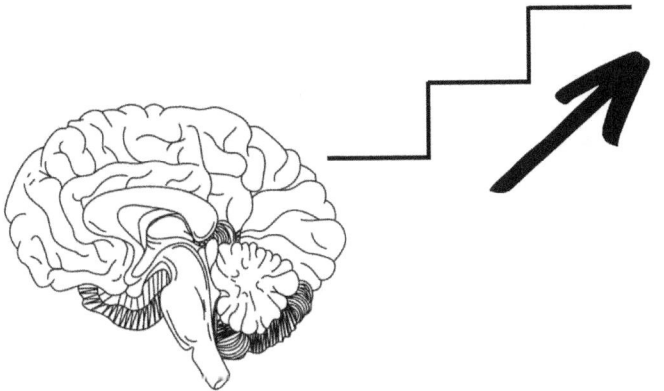

Step 3: Use assessment data to check for understanding and as an assessment tool that informs future curricular decisions

Strategies: Cognitivism

Teaching the Content	Assignments	Assessments
• uses background knowledge/cultural responsiveness to guide instruction • recognition and use of multiple intelligences with an emphasis on logistic, linguistic, and visual approaches • dynamic chunked lectures (no more than forty-five minutes at a time) • or, content is taught using consistent approaches other than lecturing Examples: • case study analyses related to the content student presentations • grouped student work • role-play	• journaling "the what, so what, now what?" • historical document analyses • case study analyses • jigsaw activities • puzzles • debates • research papers • presentations • projects (i.e., create a mock design, or a visual representation of a concept) • surveys • data collection • graphic organizers (i.e., Venn diagrams, bubble maps, concept maps, infographic)	• Formative • quizzes • observations written responses discussions games • Summative • presentations • portfolios • research essays • examinations • graphic organizers • critiques • speeches • debates • projects

COGNITIVISM: TEACHING THE CONTENT, EXAMPLE 1, THE DYNAMIC LECTURE

The Dynamic Lecture Sequence (Two-Hour Course Session)

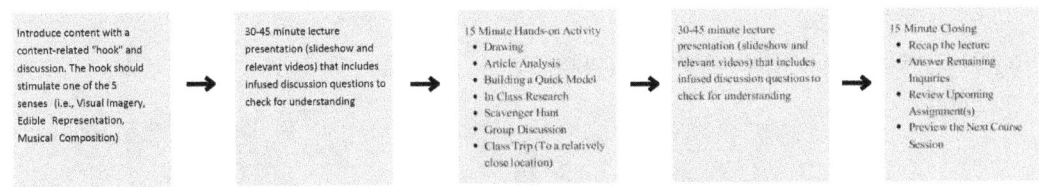

COGNITIVISM: TEACHING THE CONTENT, EXAMPLE 2, URBAN SKETCHING

To cultivate observation and critical thinking skills of real-world context specific to one's local community, urban sketching can be a helpful strategy to teach a targeted concept.

Step 1: Choose a course outcome and course topic.

Step 2: Connect the course outcome and course topic to an aspect of the local community (think about the area, structure, historical origins, immigration, worker laws, attractions, and so on.

Step 3: Create essential questions that probe critical thinking about the community and your course topic (i.e., *How does the architecture influence society, the community, . . . you?* or *How does the community connect to your local heritage?*).

Step 4: Visit a chosen community location, and facilitate students in observing the features that are significant and relevant to both *them* and the course topic.

Step 5: Facilitate students in documenting (sketching/notetaking their observations in a journal, sketchbook, or notepad).

Step 6: Assess this strategy by facilitating students in creating mock-newspaper articles, exhibitions, research papers, and so on, using what they observed and documented in the community.

COGNITIVISM: TEACHING THE CONTENT, EXAMPLE 2, URBAN SKETCHING (CONTINUED) RESOURCES

Resources

- Perspective App? Easily teaches kids perspective for $8.99 the Urban Sketcher (a technique book) $20.42 on Amazon
- https://citizensketcher.files.wordpress.com/2015/07/making-expressive-pen- and-ink-drawings-on-location.pdf (FREE)

Helpful Techniques to Cover Before Conducting the Urban Sketches

- still life drawing and figure drawing
- documenting observations
- three-pass sketch (big shapes, value, super contrast); sketch sprint (five—minute speed drawing exercises)
- visual literacy https://visualliteracytoday.org/discover-visual-literacy/

COGNITIVISM: ASSIGNMENT EXAMPLE 1, HISTORICAL DOCUMENT ANALYSES

Facilitating students in analyzing historical documents can build on their prior knowledge of a concept while enhancing their abilities to think independently and abstractly.

Inform the students:

For each module, you will be presented with two or three concepts. (See course schedule.)

1st—Read the required text chapter readings on each concept.
2nd—Choose one of the concepts to focus on.
3rd—Find at least three primary sources written by that theorist/creator of the chosen concept
4th—In a two-page paper, conduct a historical text analysis that synthesizes each of your chosen primary sources. See www.carleton.edu/history/resources/history-study-guides/primary/.

COGNITIVISM: ASSIGNMENT EXAMPLE 2, CONCEPT MAP

One strategy to facilitate students in learning new content is to have them identify and frame a problem of practice related to the content.

Inform the Students:

Create a conceptual framework that visualizes (names and frames) a problem of practice related to the concept of X. The framework is essentially an organization chart that webs the subtopics related to a topic. These subtopics would include the population effected, relevant data, theories, and theorists that address the topic, historical context, implications, naysayers, and so on. An example of this is provided below.

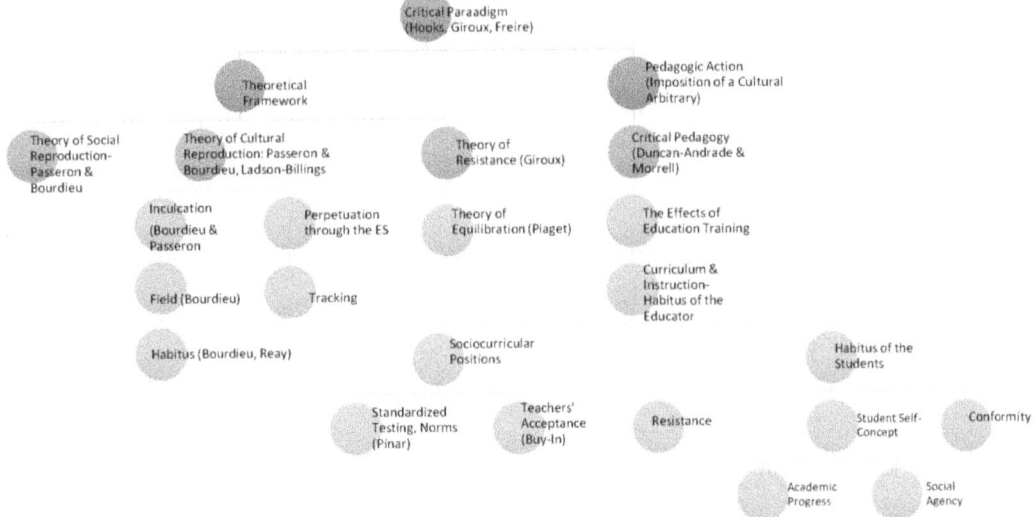

COGNITIVISM: ASSESSMENT EXAMPLE, RESEARCH ESSAY

Critical thinking is the ability to take a problem or information in general, and break it down, conceptualize it, synthesize it, and mentally manipulate the information to connect dots or create resolutions. Therefore, a research essay provides an opportunity for a professor to assess a student's critical thinking skills on one or more topics.

Before sending students off to complete this assessment, create prompts like the ones below to facilitate your students in the "how-to" of composing a research paper (to clarify your expectations).

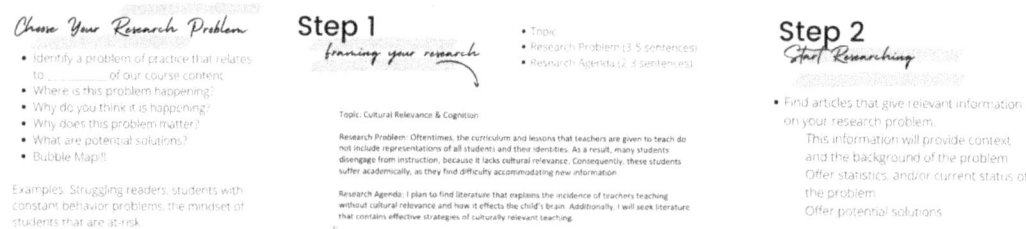

Choose Your Research Problem

- Identify a problem of practice that relates to _____ of our course content
- Where is this problem happening?
- Why do you think it is happening?
- Why does this problem matter?
- What are potential solutions?
- Bubble Map!!!

Examples: Struggling readers, students with constant behavior problems, the mindset of students that are at-risk

Step 1
framing your research

- Topic
- Research Problem (3-5 sentences)
- Research Agenda (2-3 sentences)

Topic: Cultural Relevance & Cognition

Research Problem: Oftentimes, the curriculum and lessons that teachers are given to teach do not include representations of all students and their identities. As a result, many students disengage from instruction, because it lacks cultural relevance. Consequently, these students suffer academically, as they find difficulty accommodating new information.

Research Agenda: I plan to find literature that explains the incidence of teachers teaching without cultural relevance and how it effects the child's brain. Additionally, I will seek literature that contains effective strategies of culturally relevant teaching.

Step 2
Start Researching

- Find articles that give relevant information on your research problem.
  This information will provide context and the background of the problem
  Offer statistics, and/or current status of the problem
  Offer potential solutions

Cognitivism: Assessment Example, Research Essay, Continued

Step 3
Synthesize

- Read the articles that you feel offer important contexts to your research problem
- Synthesize what you have read by stringing together common themes.
  - For example, of the articles that you read on the topic: **Cultural Relevance & Cognition** you notice these themes coming up multiple times in your articles: SEL, Assimilation, Equilibration, Identity.
  - Synthesize that information

Step 4
Synthesize cont'd.

- Create a table of these themes/subtopics
- Jot down specific takeaways that all of your articles seem to suggest about these themes. Additionally jot down differences found regarding these themes.

	Author	Main Take-Away & Argument	Counterarguments	Additional Notes
SEL				
Equilibration				
Assimilation				
Identity				

Step 5
Rough Draft

- Bubble Map Again!!! I would bubble map as a way to structure your paragraphs
- Then...Write
  - Each subtopic should include more than one paragraph of synthesis

Example 1.1 Unsuccessful synthesis: "Ormrod (1975) wrote that meaningful work builds upon life experiences and links new knowledge with previous experiences. Meaningful work contributes to a student's confidence (Bandura, 1997). Meaningful work meets an immediate need (Rogers, 2000). Seifert (2004) claimed that meaningful work contributes to a student's confidence. Finally, Craft (2003) stated that reflective journals can be meaningful tasks for the student" (p. 3).

Example 1.2 Successful synthesis: "Given the importance of meaningful learning in increasing student motivation and task persistence (Bandura, 1997; Craft, 2003; Ormrod, 1979; Rogers, 2000; Seifert, 2004), it is important to provide relevant and practical clinical teaching to clients" (p. 3).

Step 6
Final Draft

- Check for flow
- Check to see if your stance was made and supported by evidence in the research
- Proofread!
  - Maybe get someone in your family to go over it
  - APA
  - Plagiarism
- Submit

Cognitivism: Assessment Example, Research Essay, Continued

Inform the Students:

- Identify a research problem related to what we have learned concerning X.
- Using five to seven peer-reviewed articles on your research problem, write an essay (also known as a literature review) that critically thinks about the research problem that you have chosen by synthesizing peer-reviewed research. The essay must include (holistic rubric): At least five pages, not including your references with the following information:
  - Introduction paragraph: present background information on the research problem and your stance on that problem.
  - Body paragraphs (at least four and a half pages): a synthesis of articles that you researched that support and/or counter your position on the research problem. Remember to identify themes in your research and use those themes to break down your essay.
  - Conclusion (at least two paragraphs): restate the purpose of your essay and summarize your findings.

Strategies: Constructivism

Uses background knowledge and critical understandings of social needs to guide instruction
• field experiences that emphasize students' realities
  • project-based learning
  • self-discovery
  • exploration
• social interactions are emphasized
• study groups
• experimentation
• role-playing
• inquiry-based discussions
• contemporary issues discussions
• chunked lectures (no more than forty-five minutes at a time)
	• projects that solve problems
	  • identifying problems of practice
	  • data mining
	  • planning designs
	• experiments
	• assembling structures
	• peer reviews
	• jigsaw
	• activities
	• presentations
	• critiques
	• debates
	• master hour
		Formative
		• quizzes
		• observations
		• written responses
		• discussions
		• games
		Summative
		• presentations
		• portfolio
		• research papers
		• examinations
		• graphic organizers
		• critiques
		• speeches
		• debates
		• projects

Curriculum Map: Constructivism

Curriculum Map: Constructivism

Step 4: Create multiple opportunities for students to learn in the field, through social interaction and self-discovery, and critical problem solving

Step 1: Using the program outcomes and course outcomes, identify relevant real-world applications that align with them

Step 2: Identify the endgame...

Step 3: What types of student-made designs might address a local need through critical thinking and exploration

the what, so what, and now what?

Step 1: Using the program outcomes and course outcomes, identify relevant real-world applications that align with them.

Step 2: Identify the endgame . . .

Step 3: What types of student-made designs might address a local need through critical thinking and exploration?

Step 4: Create multiple opportunities for students to learn in the field, through social interaction and self-discovery, and critical problem-solving.

CONSTRUCTIVISM: TEACHING THE CONTENT, EXAMPLE 1, DEBATE

Facilitating students in debate sessions can help them essentially learn the content without direct instruction because successful debates involve research preparation, practice, critical thinking, deductive reasoning, self-discovery, and student voice. Consider using debates in multiple course sessions to strengthen these skills and vary how the content is taught.

Leading up to the debate:

- Facilitate students in the process of deductive reasoning and argumentation. Essentially communication is an argument because as humans, we are almost always declaring something when we communicate. Even in silence, we make a declarative statement.
- Use political debate clips as a source to analyze effective and fallacious arguments (arguments that are built on false privileges or inherently false justifications for the premise). Strong arguments include a logical deductive reasoned sequence:

$A = B$ and $B = C$, then $A = C$.

- Present a debate topic related to the course content. The topic should have a clear opposing and affirmative stance.
- Randomly assign the students to the opposing or affirmative stance.

CONSTRUCTIVISM: TEACHING THE CONTENT, EXAMPLE 1, DEBATE (CONTINUED)

Debate Structure

Action	Time Allowed
Introduce your stance, state your premise, provide three points of evidence to justify it, and state a counterargument to the opposing premise.	three minutes
Listen to the other side's premise/evidence and provide a rebuttal to the evidence that they provided using additional evidence that you have researched.	two minutes
Repeat the last step.	two minutes
Make closing argument.	one minute

CONSTRUCTIVISM: TEACHING THE CONTENT, EXAMPLE 1, DEBATE (CONTINUED) PEER REVIEW SCORE

Peer Review Score

Debate Components	Score
Persuasive language used	/5
Deductive reasoning of premise	/5
Use of time	/5
Rebuttal response effectiveness	/5

CONSTRUCTIVISM: TEACHING THE CONTENT, EXAMPLE 2, MASTER HOUR

The essential objective of this project is to enhance student empowerment and activate critical and divergent thinking.

- To deepen an understanding, facilitate students in selecting a course topic that they are passionate about and allow them to explore that topic during "Master Hour." Master Hour can be conducted to teach the content in place of traditional lecture approaches.
- Students will develop an inquiry question about this topic, research it, and plan a project with a culminating creatively visual presentation to share with classmates. Students will assume roles such as author, video game creator, piano teacher, instructional film producer, cupcake artist, rocket designer, architect, sports illustrator, website designer, visual-social activism, and visual historian.
- Products will include: short instructional videos, websites, public service campaigns, howto books, graphic novels, presentations of paintings, drawings, photographs, rocket and how-to presentation, models, and online video games.

CONSTRUCTIVISM: ASSIGNMENTS, EXAMPLE 1, SURVEY DATA COLLECTION

Students can further their understanding of the course content by collecting survey data on a relevant issue as an assignment and analyzing the findings. Additionally, data collection can inform additional implications and inferences of a problem.

Step 1: Discuss the three main types of survey collection

- *Descriptive*
  This survey type is used to garner quantitative data on the perceptions or nominal values of a targeted population to categorize them.
- *Exploratory*
  This survey type is used to garner qualitative (text-based) responses to perceptual questions for an understanding of *why*.
- *Correlational*
  This survey type is used to garner the strength of the relationships between variables.

Step 2: Facilitate students in collecting survey data on a problem that they have identified in their local context.

- The data should be collectible within a defined time period and relevant to the course content. Students may collect data online, over the phone, face-to-face or via email

Step 3: After survey data has been collected, have students analyze their data using statistical analysis software and write up a report of their findings and implications

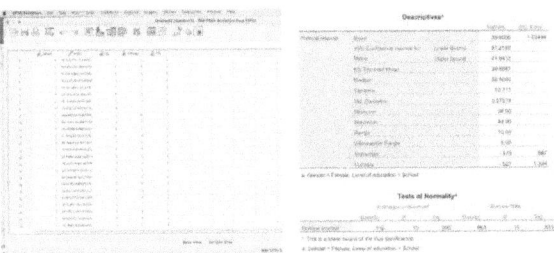

Data Analysis Instructions

- Use statistical analysis software to run descriptive, exploratory, or correlational tests
- What does the data tell you about the problem that you investigated?
- What additional data might be needed to further your analysis?
- Create a report that includes outcome graphs and charts from the tests that you ran to analyze the data and paragraphical information that explains your statistical take-aways of each.

CONSTRUCTIVISM: ASSIGNMENTS, EXAMPLE 2, MOCK UP

A mock-up is a prototype of a design idea. Having students create a mockup of a design concept that serves to solve a problem that they have identified is an effective approach to cultivating problem-solving skills. For this assignment, have students create a mock-up that reflects a solution to a problem that they have identified.

Example Mock-Up Approaches:

- clay models
- papier mâché models
- sculpting wire models
- cardboard models
- textile models
- graphically designed models

Example Mock-Up Needs:

- architecture
- hand tools
- machinery
- fashion
- web applications
- culinary
- personal devices
- medications

CONSTRUCTIVISM: ASSESSMENT, EXAMPLE 1, ADVOCACY STATEMENT

An advocacy statement is a statement that essentially identifies a problem that affects a group of people (typically a group that has been marginalized in some way), frames the problem by providing background context, and advocates for potential strategies that address that problem. Essentially, the advocacy statement briefly names, frames, and solves a problem regarding a specific population.

Inform Students:

Identify a problem related to our coursework that affects and influences a population of people. Write a two- to three-page advocacy statement that articulates the problem and advocates for specific culturally sound and professional practices.

CONSTRUCTIVISM: ASSESSMENT, EXAMPLE 1, ADVOCACY STATEMENT (CONTINUED)

Example Analytical Rubric for the Advocacy Statement

Criteria	Possible Points	Earned Points
Criterion I Questions: Clear Articulation of the Problem Clearly define the problem? Address, how does this issue impact people in the setting you chose? Address, what does current research say about this issue?	9 pts.	
Criterion II Questions: Addressing the Issue What does the research say in regard to culturally sound and professional measures for addressing this issue? What are specific actions that you can take to become a stronger advocate in regard to this issue? How do the practices you have researched and your proposed actions take into account the social, emotional, and physical needs of the population that you advocated for?	9 pts.	
Overall Quality of Work (i.e., grammar, organization, etc.)	2 pts.	
Total Points	20 pts.	

Additional Comments:

CONSTRUCTIVISM: ASSESSMENT, EXAMPLE 1, THE EXHIBITION

Exhibitions provide students with the opportunity to showcase, explain, and sometimes defend their work. To bring your students' hard work to a culminating point, having them exhibit their final projects and explorations is very effective. Additionally, doing so stimulates their self-efficacy and self-concept while also allowing them to contribute significantly to their field of study.

Types of Exhibitions:

- college/university symposiums and conferences
- local primary school showcasings
- local coffee shops
- galleries museums
- professional workshops
- the classroom (gallery walks, presentations, persuasive speeches, etc.)

NOTES

1. John Bransford, Ann Brown, and Rodney Cocking, eds., *How People Learn: Brain, Mind, Experience, and School* (Washington, DC: National Academy Press, 2000), 155–56.

2. Robert Sylwester, *A Celebration of Neurons: An Educator's Guide to the Human Brain* (Alexandria, VA: Association for Supervision and Curriculum Development, 1995), 23–24.

3. National Academies of Sciences, Engineering, and Medicine, *How People Learn II: Learners, Contexts, and Cultures* (Washington, DC: National Academies Press, 2018), 6, https://doi.org/10.17226/24783; citing the work of Draganski et al. and Lovden et al. The National Academies wrote: "This research emphasizes that a core mechanism of learning—the brain's ability to modify its connections on the basis of new experiences—functions effectively throughout the life span"; Bogdan Draganski, Christian Gaser, Volker Busch, Gerhard Schuirer, Ulrich Bogdahn, and Arne May, "Neuroplasticity: Changes in Grey Matter Induced by Training," *Nature* 427, no. 6972 (2004): 311–12, https://doi.org/10.1038/427311a; Martin Lovden, Nils Bodammer, Simon Kuhn, Jorn Kaufmann, Hartmut Schutze, Claus Tempelmann, Hans-Yochen Heinze, Emrah Duzerl, Florian Schmiedek, and Ulman Lindenberger, "Experience-Dependent Plasticity of White-Matter Microstructure Extends into Old Age," *Neuropsychologia* 48, no. 13 (2010): 3878–83, https://doi.org/10.1016/j.neuropsychologia.2010.08.026.

4. Eric Jensen and Liesl McConchie, *Brain-Based Learning: Teaching the Way Students Really Learn* (Thousand Oaks, CA: Corwin, 2020), 87. Here, the authors make special note about "coherent construction. . . . Our brains are constructing our new learning. That suggests we are mindful in the process. But unless what we piece together . . . has some meaning, it is not likely to make sense, be valuable, or be recalled" (87).

5. Jane Healy, *Your Child's Growing Mind: Brain Development and Learning from Birth to Adolescence* (New York: Broadway Books, 2007), 217.

6. Ken Bain, *What the Best College Teachers Do* (Cambridge, MA: Harvard University Press, 2004), 18.

7. Robert Sylwester, *A Celebration of Neurons: An Educator's Guide to the Human Brain* (Alexandria, VA: Association for Supervision and Curriculum Development, 1995), 72. Sylwester went on to caution: "By separating emotion from logic and reason in the classroom, we've simplified school management and evaluation, but we've also then separated two sides of one coin—and lost something important in the process. It's impossible to separate emotion from the important activities of life" (75).

8. Laurie Materna, *Jump Start the Adult Learner: How to Engage and Motivate Adults Using Brain-Compatible Strategies* (Thousand Oaks, CA: Corwin Press, 2007), 10. Materna added that the best instruction provides challenging activities. But even more important is the fact that when learning is pleasant, the material is more likely to move into long-term memory, while negative experiences force the middle brain which is responsible for emotion to downshift to the primitive parts of the brain responsible for fight or flight.

9. Jensen and McConchie, *Brain-Based Learning*, 128.

10. Paulo Freire, *Pedagogy of the Oppressed* (New York: Continuum International Publishing, 1970).

11. Healy, *Your Child's Growing Mind*, 243.

12. National Academies, *How People Learn II*, 117. Here, the Academies cited the research by Erika Patall, Harris Cooper, and Susan Wynn, "The Effectiveness and Relative Importance of Choice in the Classroom," *Journal of Educational Psychology* 102, no. 4 (2010): 896–915. The National Academies elaborated: "Self-determination theory posits that behavior is strongly influenced by three universal, innate, psychological needs—autonomy (the urge to control one's own life), competence (the urge to experience mastery), and psychological relatedness (the urge to interact with, be connected to, and care for others)" (115).

13. Bransford et al., *How People Learn*, 61.

14. Jensen and McConchie, *Brain-Based Learning*, 138–40.

15. Abraham Maslow, "A Theory of Human Motivation," *Psychological Review* 50, no. 4 (July 1943): 370–96.

16. Sofie Loyens, Joshua Magda, and Remy Rikers, "Self-Directed Learning in Problem-Based Learning and its Relationships with Self-Regulated Learning," *Educational Psychology Review* 20, no. 4 (2008): 411–27, https://doi.org/10.1007/s10648-008-9082-7.

17. Erika Patall, "Constructing Motivation Through Choice, Interest, and Interestingness," *Journal of Educational Psychology* 105, no. 2 (2013): 522–34. https://doi.org/10.1037/a0030307.

18. Healy, *Your Child's Growing Mind*, 346. Healy expresses: "Creating an atmosphere in which *wrong answers* are viewed as a learning opportunity and where [students] are encouraged to take *intellectual risks* may be the most important factor of all" (346).

19. Bransford et al., *How People Learn*, 124.

20. Materna, *Jump Start the Adult-Learner*, 28; Robert Leamnson, *Thinking about Teaching and Learning: Developing Habits of Learning with First Year College and University Students* (Sterling, VA: Sylus Publishing, 1999), 13. Leamnson extends this reasoning: "There are two points of significance here for teachers. First, it is the multiple connections between neurons that allow perceptions and thought. . . . Second, it is experience and sensory interaction with the environment that promotes and stabilizes neural connections."

21. Suzanne Wade, William Buxton, and Michelle Kelly, "Using Think-Alouds to Examine Reader–Text Interest," *Reading Research Quarterly* 34, no. 2 (1999): 194–216, in National Academies, *How People Learn*, 114.

22. Leamnson, *Thinking about Teaching and Learning*, 78 and 81.

23. Restak, *The New Brain: How the Modern Age is Rewiring Your Brain* (Emmaus, PA: Rodale Press, 2003), 21.

24. Colin Rose, *Accelerated Learning Action Guide* (Aylesbury, Buckinghamshire, UK: Accelerated Learning Systems, 1995), in Materna. *Jump Start the Adult Learner*, 37.

25. Leamnson, *Thinking about Teaching and Learning*, 101.

26. Pam Mueller and Daniel Oppenheimer, "The Pen is Mightier than the Keyboard," *Psychological Science* 25, no. 6 (2014): 1159–68, https://doi.org/10.1177/0956797614524581.

27. Bransford et al., *How People Learn*, 42.

28. Eleanor Duckworth, *"The Having of Wonderful Ideas" and Other Essays on Teaching and Learning* (New York: Teachers College Press, Columbia University, 1987), in Bransford et al., *How People Learn*, 136: "Overall, learner-centered environments include teachers who are aware that learners construct their own meanings, beginning with the beliefs, understandings, and cultural practices they bring to the classroom. If teaching is conceived as constructing a bridge between the subject matter and the student, learner-centered teachers keep a constant eye on both ends of the bridge. The teachers attempt to get a sense of what students know and can do as well as their interests and passions—what each student knows, cares about, is able to do, and wants to do."

29. National Academies, *How People Learn II*, 7.

30. Bransford et al., *How People Learn*, 136. They elaborate: "[k]nowledge-centered environments also include an emphasis on sense-making—on helping students become metacognitive by expecting new information to make sense and asking clarification when it doesn't" (137).

31. Bransford et al., *How People Learn*, 139.

32. Michio Kaku, *The Future of the Mind: The Scientific Quest to Understand, Enhance, and Empower the Mind* (New York: Doubleday, 2014), 51. Kaku elaborates: "It seems that the one characteristic most closely associated with success in life, which has persisted over the decades, is the ability to delay gratification" (137). In citing the work of other researches, he adds to the list: a person's ability to cooperate, regulate emotions, focus attention, motivation, and persistence.

33. Healy, *Your Child's Growing Mind*, 351–52. Healy goes on to state: "One large study found that 70 percent of highly creative students were not identified as 'gifted' by IQ scores" (352).

34. Healy, *Your Child's Growing Mind*, 370.

35. Bransford et al., *How People Learn*, 139.

36. Stephen Covey, *Seven Habits of Highly Effective People* (New York: Free Press, 1989).

37. Wilbert McKeachie and Marilla Svinicki, *Teaching Tips: Strategies, Research, and Theory for College and University Teachers* (Boston: Houghton-Mifflin, 2006), 36. These authors add: "In lectures . . .

research shows that most of the material covered does not make it into students' notes or memory . . . [and] that, in discussion, students pay attention and think more actively" (36). The authors conclude:

> Now we think of knowledge as being stored in structures such as networks with linked concepts, facts, and principles. The lecture thus needs to build a bridge between what is in the students' minds and the structures in the subject matter. Metaphors, examples, and demonstrations are the elements of that bridge. . . . [Now] a typical lecture strives to present a systematic, concise summary of the knowledge to be covered in the day's assignment. . . . Now more of my lectures involve analyzing materials, formulating problems, developing hypotheses, bringing evidence to bear, criticizing and evaluating alternative solutions—revealing methods of learning and thinking and involving students in the process. (60)

38. Leamnson, *Thinking about Teaching and Learning*, 145–46.
39. National Academies, *How People Learn II*, 114.
40. Terry Flowerday, Gregory Schraw, and Joseph Stevens, "The Role of Choice and Interest in Reader Engagement," *Journal of Experimental Education* 72, no. 2 (2004): 93–114.
41. Gregory Schraw and Stephen Lehman, "Situational Interest: A Review of the Literature and Directions for Future Research," *Educational Psychology Review* 13, no. 1 (2001): 23–52, https://doi.org/10.1023/A:1009004801455.
42. Barbara Condliffe, Mary Visher, Michael Bangser Sonia Drohojowska, and Larissa Saco, "Project-Based Learning: A Literature Review" (Working Paper, 2016), https://s3-us-west-1.amazonaws.com/ler/MDRC+PBL+Literature+Review.pdf (December 2017).
43. National Academies, *How People Learn II*, 7.
44. McKeachie and Svinicki, *Teaching Tips*, 109.
45. National Academies, *How People Learn II*, 155.
46. Kaku, *The Future of the Mind*, 119.
47. McKeachie and Svinicki, *Teaching Tips*, 77.

Bibliography

Ames, Carole. "Conceptions of Motivation within Competitive and Noncompetitive Goal Structures." In *Self-related Cognitions in Anxiety and Motivation*, edited by Ralf Schwarzer, 229–45. Hillsdale, NJ: Lawrence Erlbaum Associates, 1986. Cited in: National Academies of Sciences, Engineering, and Medicine. *How People Learn II: Learners, Contexts, and Cultures*. Washington, DC: The National Academies Press, 2018: 110. https://doi.org/10.17226/24783.

Anderson, Lorin, and David Krathwohl (eds.). *A Taxonomy for Learning, Teaching, and Assessing: A Revision of Bloom's Taxonomy of Educational Objectives*. New York: Longman, 2001.

Applefield, James, Richard Huber, and Mahnaz Moallem. "Constructivism in Theory and Practice: Toward a Better Understanding." *High School Journal* 84, no. 2 (2001): 35–53.

Bailey, Toni. "Othered Forms of Knowledge: Combining Theories of Aristotle and Bourdieu to Explore Intellectual Capital in the Curriculum." *Curriculum and Teaching Dialogue* 24, nos. 1 and 2 (2022): 51–65.

Bain, Ken. *What the Best College Teachers Do*. Cambridge, MA: Harvard University Press, 2004.

Bengtsson, Sara, Zoltan Nagy, Stefan Skare, Lea Forsman, Hans Forssberg, and Fredrik Ullen, "Extensive Piano Practicing Has Regionally Specific Effects on White Matter Development," *Nature Neuroscience* 8, no. 9 (2005): 1148–50.

Benjamin, Aaron, and J. Jonathan Tullis. "What Makes Distributed Practice Effective?" *Cognitive Psychology* 61, no. 3 (2010): 228–47. https://doi.org/10.1016/j.cogpsych.2010.05.004.

Bloom, Benjamin, M. Engelhart, E. Furst, Hill, and W. Krathwohl. Taxonomy of Educational Objectives: The Classification of Educational Goals. New York: David McKay Company, 1956.

Bourdieu, Pierre. "Cultural Reproduction and Social Reproduction." In *Power and Ideology in Education*, edited by J. Karabel and A. Halsey. New York: Oxford University Press, 1977.

Bourdieu, Pierre, and Jean Claude Passeron. *Reproduction in Education, Society, and Culture*. Thousand Oaks, CA: Sage, 1990.

Bransford, John, Ann Brown, and Rodney Cocking, eds. *How People Learn: Brain, Mind, Experience, and School*. Washington, DC: National Academy Press, 2000.

Brooks, Jacqueline, and Martin Brooks. "Becoming a Constructivist Teacher." In *Developing Minds: A Resource Book for Teaching Thinking*, edited by A. L. Costa, 150–57. Alexandria, VA: ASCD, 2001.

Bueno, David. "Genetics and Learning: How the Genes Influence Educational Attainment." *Frontiers in Psychology* 10 (2019): 1–10.

Caine, Renate Nummela, and Geoffrey Caine. "Understanding a Brain-Based Approach to Learning and Teaching." *Educational Leadership*. Association for Supervision and Curriculum Development (October 1990): 66–70.

Canlas, Melissa, Amy Argenal, and Monisha Bajaj. "Teaching Human Rights from Below: Towards Solidarity, Resistance and Social Justice." *Radical Teacher* 103 (2015): 38–46.

Chang, Yongmin, "Reorganization and Plastic Changes of the Human Brain Associated with S k i l l Learning and Expertise." *Frontiers in Human Neuroscience* 8, no. 35 (2014).   https://doi.org/10.3389/fnhum.2014.00035.

Cohen, Leonora, and Younghee Kim. "Piaget's Equilibration Theory and the Young Gifted Child: A Balancing Act." *Roeper Review* 21, no. 3 (1999): 201–6. https://doi.org/10.1080/02783199909553962.

Condliffe, Barbara, Mary Visher, Michael Bangser Sonia Drohojowska, and Larissa Saco. *Project based Learning: A Literature Review* (2016): https://s3-us-west-1.amazonaws.com/ler/MDRC+PBL+Literature+Review.pdf. (December 2017).

Covey, Stephen. *Seven Habits of Highly Effective People*. New York: Free Press, 1989.

Csikszentmihalyi, Mihalyi. *Flow: The Psychology of Optimal Experience*. New York: Harper Collins, 1990.

Davies, Gail, Max Lam, Sarah Harris, Joey Trampush, Michelle Luciano, and W. David Hill. "Study of 300,486 Individuals Identifies 148 Independent Genetic Loci Influencing General Cognitive Function." *Nat Communications* 9, no. 1 (2018): 1–16.

Draganski, Bogdan, Christian Gaser, Volker Busch, Gerhard Schuirer, Ulrich Bogdahn, and Arne May. "Neuroplasticity: Changes in Grey Matter Induced by Training." *Nature* 427, no. 6972 (2004): 311–12. https://doi.org/10.1038/427311a.

Duckworth, Eleanor. *"The Having of Wonderful Ideas" and Other Essays on Teaching and Learning*. New York: Teachers College Press, Columbia University, 1987.

Dunlap, Glen, Lee Kern-Dunlap, and Jonathan Worcester. "ABA and Academic Instruction." *Focus on Autism and Other Developmental Disabilities* 16, no. 2 (2001): 130.

Ecker, K. H., Ullrich, Briony Swire, and Stephan Lewandowsky. "Correcting Misinformation—A Challenge for Education and Cognitive Science." In *Processing Inaccurate Information: Theoretical and Implied Perspectives from Cognitive Science and the Educational Sciences*, edited by David Rapp and Jason Braasch. Cambridge, MA: MIT Press, 2014.

Ertmer, Peggy, and Timothy Newby. "Behaviorism, Cognitivism, Constructivism: Comparing Critical Features from an Instructional Design Perspective." *Performance Improvement Quarterly* 6, no. 4 (1993): 50–72.

Flowerday, Terry, Gregory Schraw, and Joseph Stevens. "The Role of Choice and Interest in Reader Engagement." *The Journal of Experimental Education* 72, no. 2 (2004): 93–114.

Fostnot, Catherine Twomey. *Constructivism: Theory, Perspectives, and Practice*. New York: Teachers College Press, 2005.

Fox, Emily, and Michelle Riconscente. "Metacognition and Self-regulation in James, Piaget, and Vygotsky." *Educational Psychology Review* 20, no. 4 (2008): 373–89. https://doi.org/10.1007/s10648-008-9079-2.

Freire, Paulo. *Pedagogy of the Oppressed*. New York: Continuum International Publishing, 1970.

———. *Pedagogy of the Oppressed*. New York: Bloomsbury, 2000.

Gardner, Howard. *Multiple Intelligences*. New York: Basic Books, 1993.

Gehlbach, Hunter, Maureen Brinkworth, Aaron King, Laura Hsu, Joseph McIntyre, and Todd Rogers. "Creating Birds of Similar Feathers: Leveraging Similarity to Improve Teacher–Student Relationship and Academic Achievement." *Journal of Educational Psychology* 108, no. 3 (2016): 342–52.

Generals, Donald Jr. "The Architect of Progressive Education: John Dewey or Booker T. Washington." (2002): 186; In: National Association of African American Studies & National Association of Hispanic and Latino Studies: 2000 Literature Monograph Series. Proceedings (Education Section) (Houston, TX, February 21–26, 2000).

Gholson, Barry, Amy Witherspoon, Brent Morgan, Joshua Brittingham, Robert Coles, Arthur Graesser, Jeremiah Sullins, and Scotty Craig. "Exploring the Deep-Level Reasoning Questions Effect During Vicarious Learning among Eighth to Eleventh Graders in the Domains of Computer Literacy and Newtonian Physics. *Instructional Science* 37, no. 5 (2009): 487–93.

Giroux, Henry. *Theory and Resistance in Education: Towards a Pedagogy for the Opposition*. Westport, CT: Bergin & Garvey, 2001.

Grant, Carl, and Melissa Gibson. "The Path of Social Justice: A Human Rights History of Social Justice Education." *Equity and Excellence in Education* 46, no. 1 (2013): 81–99.

Gredler, Margaret. "Understanding Vygotsky for the Classroom: Is It Too Late?" *Educational Psychology Review* 24, no. 1 (2012): 113–31.

Greeno, James, "A Perspective on Thinking." *American Psychologist* 44, no. 2 (1989): 134–41.
Gutek, Gerald. *Historical and Philosophical Foundations of Education: A Biographical Introduction.* New York: Pearson, 2011.
Hacker, Douglas, "Failures to Detect Textual Problems During Reading." In *Processing Inaccurate Information: Theoretical and Implied Perspectives from Cognitive Science and the Educational Sciences,* edited by David Rapp and Jason Braasch, 88. Cambridge, MA: MIT Press, 2014.
Hammond, Zaretta. *Culturally Responsive Teaching and the Brain: Promoting Authentic Engagement and Rigor among Culturally and Linguistically Diverse Students.* New York: Corwin Press, 2015.
Hastings, Erin, and Robin West. "Goal Orientation and Self-Efficacy in Relation to Memory in Adulthood." *Aging, Neuropsychology, and Cognition* 18, no. 4 (2011): 471–93. https://doi.org/10.1080/13825585.2011.575926.
Healy, Jane. *Your Child's Growing Mind: Brain Development and Learning from Birth to Adolescence.* New York: Broadway Books, 2007.
Holecek, Andrew. *Dream Yoga: Illuminating Your Life through Lucid Dreaming and the Tibetan Yogas of Sleep.* Boulder, CO: Sounds True, 2016.
Holmes, Geraldine, and Michele Abington-Cooper. "Pedagogy vs. Andragogy: A False Dichotomy." *Journal of Technology Studies* 26, no. 2 (2000): para. 3.
Immordino-Yang, Mary Helen, and Rebecca Gotlieb. "Embodied Brains, Social Minds, Cultural Meaning: Integrating Neuroscientific and Educational Research on Social-Affective Development." *American Educational Research Journal: Centennial Issue* 54, no. 1 (2017): 344S–67S. http://journals.sagepub.com/doi/abs/10.3102/0002831216669780.
Institute of Medicine. *From Neurons to Neighborhoods: The Science of Early Childhood Development.* Washington, DC: National Academy Press, 2000.
Jensen, Eric, and Liesl McConchie. *Brain-Based Learning: Teaching the Way Students Really Learn.* Thousand Oaks, CA: Corwin, 2020.
Kaku, Michio. *The Future of the Mind: The Scientific Quest to Understand, Enhance, and Empower the Mind.* New York: Doubleday, 2014.
Knowles, Malcolm. *The Adult Learner: A Neglected Species.* Houston: Gulf Publishing, 1973.
Leamnson, Robert. *Thinking about Teaching and Learning: Developing Habits of Learning with First Year College and University Students.* Sterling, VA: Sylus Publishing, 1999.
Leisman, Gerry, Raed Mualem, and Safa Khayat Mughrabi. "The Neurological Development of the Child with the Educational Enrichment in Mind." *Psicología Educativa* 21, no. 2 (2015): 79–96. https://doi.org/10.1016/j.pse.2015.08.006.
Lenroot, Rhosel, and Jay Giedd. "Brain Development in Children and Adolescents: Insights from Anatomical Magnetic Resonance Imaging." *Neuroscience Biobehavioral Review* 30, no. 6 (2006): 718–29.
Levitin, Daniel. *This is Your Brain on Music: The Science of a Human Obsession.* New York: Plume of Penguin Group, 2006.
Lichtman, Marilyn. *Qualitative Research in Education: A User's Guide,* third edition. Thousand Oaks, CA: Sage, 2013.
Lovden, Martin, Nils Bodammer, Simon Kuhn, Jorn Kaufmann, Hartmut Schutze, Claus Tempelmann, Hans-Yochen Heinze, Emrah Duzerl, Florian Schmiedek, and Ulman Lindenberger. "Experience-Dependent Plasticity of White-Matter Microstructure Extends into Old Age." *Neuropsychologia* 48, no. 13 (2010): 3878–83. https://doi.org/10.1016/j.neuropsychologia.2010.08.026.
Loyens, Sofie, Joshua Magda, and Remy Rikers. "Self-Directed Learning in Problem-Based Learning and Its Relationships with Self-Regulated Learning." *Educational Psychology Review* 20, no. 4 (2008): 411–27. https://doi.org/10.1007/s10648-008-9082-7.
Marzano, Robert, and John Kendall. *The New Taxonomy of Educational Objectives.* Thousand Oaks, CA: Corwin Press, 2006.
Maslow, Abraham. "A Theory of Human Motivation." *Psychological Review* 50, no. 4 (July 1943): 370–96.

Materna, Laurie. *Jump Start the Adult Learner: How to Engage and Motivate Adults Using Brain-Compatible Strategies*. Thousand Oaks, CA: Corwin Press, 2007.

McKeachie, Wilbert, and Marilla Svinicki. *Teaching Tips: Strategies, Research, and Theory for College and University Teachers*. Boston: Houghton-Mifflin, 2006.

McMahon, Brenda. "Putting the Elephant into the Refrigerator: Student Engagement, Critical Pedagogy and Antiracist Education." *McGill Journal of Education* 38, no. 2 (2003): 257–73.

Medaglia, John, Mary-Ellen Lynall, and Danielle Bassett. "Cognitive Network Neuroscience." *Journal of Cognitive Neuroscience* 27, no. 8 (2015): 1471–91.

Mueller, Pam, and Daniel Oppenheimer. "The Pen is Mightier than the Keyboard." *Psychological Science* 25, no. 6 (2014): 1159–68. https://doi.org/10.1177/0956797614524581.

National Academies of Sciences, Engineering, and Medicine. *How People Learn II: Learners, Contexts, and Cultures*. Washington, DC: National Academies Press, 2018. https://doi.org/10.17226/24783.

National Research Council. *Education for Life and Work: Developing Transferable Knowledge and Skills in the 21st Century*. Washington, DC: National Academies Press, 2012.

National Research Council and Institute of Medicine. *Transforming the Workforce for Children Birth Through Age 8: A Unifying Foundation*. Washington, DC: National Academies Press, 2015.

Ormrod, Jane Ellis, and Brett Jones. *Essentials of Educational Psychology*. New York: Pearson, 2019.

Parker, Charles. "Professor Charles I. Parker, of Chicago, Answers the Question, 'Have We too Many Examinations?'" *The Daily Inter-Ocean* (January 11, 1878): 6.

Patall, Erika. "Constructing Motivation Through Choice, Interest, and Interestingness." *Journal of Educational Psychology* 105, no. 2 (2013): 522–34. https://doi.org/10.1037/a0030307.

Patall, Erika, Harris Cooper, and Susan Wynn. "The Effectiveness and Relative Importance of Choice in the Classroom." *Journal of Educational Psychology* 102, no. 4 (2010): 896–915.

Piaget, Jean. *The Development of Thought: Equilibration of Cognitive Structures*. Presses Universitaires de France (1975). https://doi.org/10.2307/1175382. Corpus ID: 144929866.

Pinar, William. *What is Curriculum Theory?* New York: Routledge, 2004.

Rapp, David, and Jason Braasch, eds. *Processing Inaccurate Information*. Cambridge, MA: MIT Press, 2014.

Restak, Richard. *The New Brain: How the Modern Age is Rewiring Your Brain*. Emmaus, Pennsylvania: Rodale Press, 2003.

Rimfeld, Kaili, Ziada Ayorech, Philip Dale, Yulia Kovas, and Robert Plomin. "Genetics Affects Choice of Academic Subjects as well as Achievement." *Scientific Reports* 6 (2016): 1–9.

Rose, Colin. *Accelerated Learning Action Guide*. Aylesbury, Buckinghamshire, UK: Accelerated Learning Systems, 1995.

Schraw, Gregory, and Stephen Lehman. "Situational Interest: A Review of the Literature and Directions for Future Research." *Educational Psychology Review* 13, no. 1 (2001): 23–52. https://doi.org/10.1023/A:1009004801455.

Schunk, Dale. *Learning Theories: An Educational Perspective*. New York: Pearson, 2012.

Schwarzer, Ralf, ed. *Self-related Cognitions in Anxiety and Motivation*. Hillsdale, NJ: Lawrence Erlbaum Associates, 1986.

Seifert, Colleen. "The Continued Influence Effect: The Persistence of Misinformation in Memory and Reasoning Following Correction." In *Processing Inaccurate Information: Theoretical and Implied Perspectives from Cognitive Science and the Educational Sciences*, edited by David Rapp and Jason Braasch, 39. Cambridge, MA: MIT Press, 2014.

Shlain, Leonard. *The Alphabet Versus the Goddess: The Conflict Between Word and Image*. New York: Penguin Group, 1998.

Skinner, B. F. "The Shame of American Education" *American Psychologist* 39, no. 9 (1984): 947–54.

———. "Whatever Happened to Psychology as the Science of Behavior?" *American Psychologist* 42, no. 8 (1987): 780–86.

Sporns, Olaf. *Networks of the Brain*. Cambridge, MA: MIT Press, 2011.

Spring, Joel. *Deculturalization and the Struggle for Equality*. New York: McGraw-Hill, 1997.

Sylwester, Robert. *A Celebration of Neurons: An Educator's Guide to the Human Brain.* Alexandria, VA: Association for Supervision and Curriculum Development, 1995.

Talbot, Michael. *The Holographic Universe.* New York: Harper Collins, 1991.

Thompson, Evan. *Waking, Dreaming, Being: Self and Consciousness in Neuroscience, Meditation, and Philosophy.* New York: Columbia University Press, 2017.

Thorndike, Edward. *Animal Intelligence: Experimental Studies.* New York: Macmillan, 1911.

Tolman, Edward. "Instinct and Purpose," *Psychological Review* 27, no. 3 (1920): 217–33.

Tracy, Sarah J., *Qualitative Research Methods.* West Sussex, UK: Wiley-Blackwell, 2013.

Wade, Suzanne, William Buxton, and Michelle Kelly. "Using Think-Alouds to Examine Reader–Text Interest." *Reading Research Quarterly* 34, no. 2 (1999): 194–216.

Washington, Booker T. "Principal's Annual Report." Unpublished manuscript. Tuskegee Institute. *BTW Papers*, Library of Congress, 1902, https://lccn.loc.gov/mm78044669.

Watson, John B. "What the Nursery Has to Say about Instincts." In *Psychologies of 1925*, edited by Carl Murchinson, 1–35. Worcester, MA: Clark University Press, 1926). https://psycnet.apa.org/doi/10.1037/11020-001.

Wiggins, Grant, and Jay McTighe. *Understanding by Design.* Alexandria, VA: Association for Supervision and Curriculum Development, 2005.

Williams, Raymond. *Culture and Society 1780–1950.* London, UK: Chatto and Windus, 1958.

Wolf, Fred Alan. *The Dreaming Universe: A Mind-Expanding Journey into the Realm Where Psyche and Physics Meet.* New York: Touchstone, 1994.

Yilmaz, Kaya. "The Cognitive Perspective on Learning: Its Theoretical Underpinnings and Implications for Classroom Practices." Clearing House: A Journal of Educational Strategies, Issues and Ideas 84, no. 5 (2011): 204–12.

Zakin, Andrea. "Metacognition and the Use of Inner Speech in Children's Thinking: A Tool Teachers Can Use." *Journal of Education and Human Development* 1, no. 2 (2007): 1–14. https://doi.org/10.1037/0003-066X.34.10.906.

Annotated Bibliography

While dozens of books and articles were central to the writing of this book, the following played a significant role and should be considered for any university's center for teaching and learning, or CTL.

Bain, Ken. *What the Best College Teachers Do*. Cambridge, MA: Harvard University Press, 2004.

>Most college centers for teaching and learning already have this book on file. If they don't, they need to do so. Bain has researched this topic for years and now shares his experiences and his research with the readers. The book is a quick read with immediate application for every professor's classroom.

Bransford, John, Ann Brown, and Rodney Cocking, eds. *How People Learn: Brain, Mind, Experience, and School*. Washington, DC: National Academy Press, 2000.

>This book is exceptionally well written and focuses exclusively on learning theory and implications for the K–12 classroom. It is thorough and detailed, yet it gives direct implications primarily for the K–12 setting. Like other such books, however, the implications and applications are relevant for instructors at any level. It is written by professional educators for professional educators.

Breslaw, Elaine. "Behaviorism in the Classroom." *Change: The Magazine of Higher Learning* 5, no. 3 (1973): 52–55.

>This article provides a rare account of how behaviorism can be directly applied to a college or university classroom. Its application is unique, though, not only because of its rarity, but because it emphasizes the idea that behaviorism is not just a strict and mundane perspective of how we learn, it is essentially the basis of rhythmic and scheduled patterns that occur in so many aspects of our everyday lives, and to a great degree are appreciated.

Bueno, David. "Genetics and Learning: How the Genes Influence Educational Attainment." *Frontiers in Psychology* 10 (2019): 1–10.

>This article provides a comprehensive explanation of how educators can influence their students' biological functions through the classroom environment that they establish. Scientific evidence is provided to conclude that genetic traits have been traced to environmental influences. Therefore, the ability to reason or create can be relatively correlated with the degree to which an educator has structured their classroom environment to nurture and optimize those abilities.

Gardner, Howard. *Frames of Mind: The Theory of Multiple Intelligences*. New York: Basic Books, 1983.

The idea that students learn contingent upon specific learning modalities has been a bit of a point of contention in the field of education. This text provides a convincing argument that our concept of intelligence is contingent upon societal norms. However, if we broaden our scope, we can instead view intelligence as a system of codes or languages that can be transferrable to most learners when they are aware that different learning modalities exist and are taught in a variety of ways that align with them.

Gutek, Gerald. *Historical and Philosophical Foundations of Education: A Biographical Introduction.* New York: Pearson, 2011.

This text provides a comprehensive account of curriculum, from its earliest beginnings to modern day practices. With roughly 2,500 years of curriculum theories, Gutek gives a thorough understanding of each curricular movement and the societal contexts that invoked those movements.

Hammond, Zaretta. *Culturally Responsive Teaching and the Brain: Promoting Authentic Engagement and Rigor among Culturally and Linguistically Diverse Students.* Thousand Oaks, CA: Corwin Press, 2015.

This text introduces culturally responsive teaching through a neurological lens. It provides an in-depth yet digestible overview of achievement disparities, functions of the brain, and the critical role that culturally responsive teaching plays in cognitive processes. This text is very useful for all types of educators and could even extend to leadership roles outside of education as well.

Holmes, Geraldine, and Michele Abington-Cooper. "Pedagogy vs. Andragogy." *Journal of Technology Studies* 26, no. 2 (2000): para. 3.

This article provides an oppositional analysis of the pedagogy vs andragogy debate. It provides a wide understanding of arguments from both camps and offers a thoughtful resolution for reconciling them.

Healy, Jane. *Your Child's Growing Mind: Brain Development and Learning from Birth to Adolescence.* New York: Broadway Books, 2007.

This book is an exceptional read for anyone seeking to understand how children learn and how best to teach them. Its primary audience might seem to be parents, but all audiences will find it relevant. If you are looking for an extremely thorough understanding of the brain's growth and development, this is a must-read, and it's written in laymen terms.

Jensen, Eric, and Liesl McConchie. *Brain-Based Learning: Teaching the Way Students Really Learn.* Thousand Oaks, CA: Corwin, 2020.

Eric Jensen has written numerous books about brain research and its implications for K–12 student populations. Each book is equally relevant to broad audiences. This book, in particular, shares numerous examples and insights for teachers to apply brain-compatible approaches to their own classrooms.

Leamnson, Robert. *Thinking about Teaching and Learning: Developing Habits of Learning with First Year College and University Students.* Sterling, VA: Sylus Publishing, 1999.

This is another book that should be housed in every campus's center for teaching and learning. Leamnson provides an erudite examination of how young college students learn with practical application that can be implemented immediately. This is a very thoughtful read and should be part of any CTL book study for serious professors.

Materna, Laurie. *Jump Start the Adult Learner: How to Engage and Motivate Adults Using Brain-Compatible Strategies*. Thousand Oaks, CA: Corwin Press, 2007.

This book is very user friendly and is one of the only books of its kind devoted to the adult learner. It provides plenty of real-life classroom examples from Dr. Materna's own teaching experience. While she writes from a Nursing professor viewpoint, the examples are relevant to all content areas. It is an essential book for all CTLs.

McKeachie, Wilbert, and Marilla Svinicki. *Teaching Tips: Strategies, Research, and Theory for College and University Teachers*. Boston: Houghton-Mifflin, 2006.

Like other books dedicated to college professors, *Teaching Tips* belongs in every center for teaching and learning. It not only covers a broad range of implications and applications across content areas but does so in a very pragmatic and user-friendly manner. The ideas that are shared can be put in place immediately.

Ormrod, Jane Ellis, and Brett Jones. *Essentials of Educational Psychology*, fifth edition. New York: Pearson, 2019.

Dr. Rettig and Dr. Bailey have used this book in their undergraduate and graduate courses for learning and cognition. It is thoroughly researched and written for college and graduate students. While it is written to explain K–12 learners, it has general applicability for wider audiences. Certainly, every school of education should have this book in its library.

Schunk, Dale. *Learning Theories: An Educational Perspective*. New York: Pearson, 2012.

This book provides a foundational and historical account of each of the major learning theories. It is an excellent textbook for students majoring in education. However, much of this text can also be applied to learning in the college classroom as well using the theories and examples to make intentional instructional decisions.

Sylwester, Robert. *A Celebration of Neurons: An Educator's Guide to the Human Brain*. Alexandria, VA: Association for Supervision and Curriculum Development (ASCD), 1995.

While this book is old, the information is accurate and remains as relevant today as it did when it first came out. The ASCD is an exceptional organization devoted to teaching and teacher education. This book focuses primarily on the young mind, but it is relevant for the understanding of all learners.

About the Authors

Perry Rettig, PhD, started his educational career in 1984 as a public school teacher in rural Green Bay, Wisconsin. He taught fourth grade, fifth grade, fourth/fifth grade combined class, and seventh/eighth grade English and literature over a five-year span. Subsequently, he became a public school principal for seven years in Sheboygan, Wisconsin, serving at both the elementary and middle school levels.

After those initial twelve years in the K–12 setting, Rettig became a professor of educational leadership and administration. His first year of service began at Northern State University in Aberdeen, South Dakota. He then moved back to Wisconsin to serve as a professor of educational leadership and administration at the University of Wisconsin-Oshkosh. While there, he eventually served as chancellor's leadership fellow and then associate vice chancellor for academic affairs.

In 2013, he moved to Piedmont University north of Atlanta, Georgia, where he served as vice president for academic affairs. Over the next years, he also served in the roles of vice president of the Athens Campus, vice president for student affairs and enrollment management, and even served in the capacity of interim dean of nursing and health sciences and interim dean of education. In 2022 he returned to the classroom as distinguished university professor, making a full circle of his educational career.

Dr. Rettig received his bachelor's degree in education from the University of Wisconsin-Whitewater, his master's degree in educational leadership from the University of Wisconsin-Milwaukee, and his doctorate degree in educational leadership from Marquette University. This is his tenth book, his ninth with Rowman & Littlefield.

Toni Bailey, PhD, began her educational career as a first grade charter-school teacher in New Orleans, Louisiana, shortly after Hurricane Katrina devastated the area. After serving a year in that role, she became a middle school art teacher at Druid Hills Middle School in Decatur, Georgia, where she served in that role and as well as the elective department chair for nine years. Following her K–12 experience, she became an assistant professor of education in the department of advanced graduate studies at Piedmont University in Athens, Georgia.

Dr. Bailey received her bachelor's degree in fine arts from Xavier University of Louisiana, her master's degree in the art of teaching, and her doctorate degree in curriculum and instruction from Mercer University. Additionally, her research includes learning and cognition as it relates to social and cultural capital.

www.ingramcontent.com/pod-product-compliance
Lightning Source LLC
Chambersburg PA
CBHW081946230426
43669CB00019B/2942